Tatted Angels

Tatted Angels

Fay Lamb

FirstPublish, Inc.
Orlando, Florida

Scripture quotations are taken from the Holy Bible,
King James Version

ISBN
1-929925-50-6

Library of Congress Cataloging in Publication Data
00-111012

Fay Lamb
Tatted Angels

FIRSTPUBLISH, INC.
170 Sunport Ln. Suite 900
Orlando, FL 32809
407-240-1414
www.firstpublish.com

Dedication

This book is dedicated to
those I love, both family and friends,
who know first-hand that grief is an inescapable
part of being alive.

And it is written
in memory of:

ELIZABETH FAY THOMPSON
COLLEEN M. THOMPSON
AND
CONRAD BLANCHARD

Their loss created a hole in my soul
filled only by God and his
wonderful gift of allowing this story to go
from mind to page

Acknowledgements

*I*f you read this book and like it, to God be all the glory. If you find it hard to read, I take responsibility. Still, I thank the Lord for his never-ending patience with this spoiled child and for the joy of a work accomplished.

To my husband Marc, I can never fully express the love that I have for you. On July 11, 1987, I met my soul mate and my best friend. You are and have made my every dream come true.

To my father and mother-in-law, Coram and Saralyn Lamb, I thank you for sharing your only son with me and for being the best in-laws and grandparents in the world.

To my friend, Bobbie Fish, your encouragement, your praise, and your prayers have given me the courage to take the steps needed to accomplish my goal.

To my pastor, Jim Nitz, I know I speak for every member of Calvary Baptist Church when I say thank you for teaching us chapter by chapter, verse by verse and for challenging us to seek the wisdom in your teaching by reading the scriptures; and

To my Aunt MaryJean, thank you for being my example of an angel on earth. You are the glue that holds the Thompson family together.

Chapter One

Tattered Dreams

"He that goeth forth and weepeth, bearing precious
seed, shall doubtless come again with rejoicing,
bringing his sheaves with him." - Psalm 126:6

"Michael," my mother once told me, "your blue eyes were filled with hope from the moment you were born, but now they seem brighter than ever."

That was a happy day for me. Walking out of the church, my parents on each side, I beamed with the Spirit inside me as we stepped onto the concrete path leading to the street. "I'm saved," I declared. My mother and father stopped their slow pace. They looked one to another. My father smiled, but my mother burst into tears. Suddenly Dad's smile vanished, and he pushed me aside. "Isn't is wonderful?" He tried to convince her.

What had I done? I thought she would be happy. Claire Abernathy never knew a worry; at least I was unaware of any. She always held faith that whatever she needed would be provided by the unseen hand of the Father above. My mother never wanted for anything, she said, except for the happiness of her only child and her loving husband. Up until this point, I was sure Dad and I never caused her any disappointment. She was our delight and life seemed easy because that was Claire's way. I was ashamed at having made Mom cry.

When she reached out suddenly and hugged me tightly to her, my thoughts quickly changed from her unhappiness to mine. She was

1

causing a scene. I could see from the churchyard that three of my friends were pointing and laughing. Jesse Crum, the preacher's son, was on his knees holding his stomach. Leaning against him for leverage so that they would not fall was my best buddy, Mickey Roberts, and Seth New.

"I'm so happy. Thank you, Lord," my mother cried against me. I was relieved that her tears were caused by happiness and not by anger or shame. I was even happier when Jesse's mother started in the direction of my friends. In a surprise attack she pinched her son's earlobe. He cried out and stood. All laughter was gone as Barbara Crum's lecture began. My mother missed the entire scene, but my father shared a smile with me. My honor was vindicated.

"This is the most important day of your life," Mom continued.

It would have pained her if I told her she was wrong. I dreamed of the all-important day when I would say goodbye to the one-horse town of my birth. Serenity Key is actually an island, a well-kept secret in a world of fast-paced life styles; at least that's what my father told me. He commented often that Serenity holds an unexplainable calmness. Even in the midst of upheaval, there is always a sense that tomorrow will come, and the sun will shine brightly through the clouds. At fourteen, though, tranquility was not a high priority. Still, I had to admit that on our island you immediately feel you belong. Strangers to our city notice it and comment about it. Long time natives take it for granted. I took it for granted.

My early years set my heart on adventure. I grew up on the island because my father tired of the lack of journalistic ethics in the larger city of Detroit. I was born in the house Trevor Abernathy purchased for his bride, Claire, and I was a child of the island, growing up along and in the waters of the Gulf. I knew how to sail before I was ten, and total exploration of the outer islands was completed before I turned twelve. I wrote my first news article for my father's paper, the *Serenity Serenade* at the tried and true age of thirteen. It was a local interest piece describing the history of Serenity's two barrier islands, Angel and Devil Keys. From that day on, I began to develop a deep yearning to experience life outside Serenity and to write about those events.

In most ways, I was definitely my father's son. I learned early how to operate the press that ran the paper. I knew words and words were my life. There were ways I was different from Trevor. I was intent on using my knowledge for a one-way ticket out of town. I wanted to write news, real news, and I reveled in thoughts of interviewing victims, of getting to the meat of a story in words and in pictures. On the other hand, Dad often remarked about the lack of journalistic integrity. He scoffed at the way a journalist pried into the lives of the various victims. He ranted and raved when they hounded defenseless family members over the loss of a loved one. He openly despised the paparazzi that made their living by invading the privacy of others.

There are others on Serenity that I know almost as well as I know myself. We attended Sunday school together, and even though a year or two may have separated us by grade, we most often were in the same small schoolroom. (No, we are not circa 1898. We are Serenity Key). Mickey Roberts always held the title of best friend. He and I were the same age, and until we turned fourteen, he had no choice but to look up to me. Then, suddenly, he grew taller by three inches, a growth I could never obtain. Mickey and I were always together. With our blonde hair, often we were mistaken for brothers, and with our names being so similar it was not always easy to convince strangers that we were not twins. Actually, Mickey's name was the same as mine. He just inherited his father's nickname. His mother was the best storyteller in town, and she was also our Sunday school teacher. Every kid in Serenity loved Sabrina Roberts. Each Saturday we would gather at the Serenity Key Library to hear her read to us. It was a magical treat to sit and watch this woman as she engrossed us in the story of the week, and every kid in church fought to be in her Sunday school class. It wasn't until after the loss of her husband that she obtained her degree and began teaching elementary school. It was the most natural thing for her to do. It was her calling.

Mickey's father had been the town's only lawyer until his death caused by his untreated diabetes. He lapsed into a coma for only one day prior to his passing. I remember vividly the day Mickey walked onto my porch. We were twelve years old. "Whatcha doing?" He leaned over me while I worked with my favorite reel, the one he utterly destroyed a day earlier by snagging it on a rock off Devil's Key. We had gone fishing at Sabrina Robert's insistence. Mickey needed a distraction, she told us. "What does it look like?" I spat. There was no answer, and I looked up intending to cast him a glare that would tell him I was angry when, in fact, I never stayed mad with Mickey for very long. He wiped his eyes with the back of his hand. I noticed that they were moist and red. His face was flushed. His lips trembled. "Dad's gone," he managed the words before he choked on his sobs. I could say nothing. We all expected Mr. Roberts to pull through. My mother was diligent in her prayers. At the dinner table the night before, we held hands and especially asked God to heal him quickly.

"You poor baby," my mother ran onto the porch. His voice was so low I didn't know how she knew he was there. I learned later that Sabrina phoned her. Their friendship caused them to share joy and pain equally, and it was Sabrina's request that my mother comfort her son before running to console her. Mickey cried against her that day. It was strange for me. I remembered thinking it didn't matter how bad things became; Mickey would never see me cry. Still, I never told anyone about his weakness. I would never embarrass him that way.

Seth New and Jesse Crum were also friends. Seth's father owns Jake's Place, a restaurant on Front Street. Seth's mother died several months after his birth, and I always felt sorry for him. I knew if I ever lost either of my parents, it would mean that life was over. Seth, though, having never known his mother, seemed not to recognize his loss.

You would never have known that Jesse Crum's father was the pastor of the Serenity Key Baptist Church, and his mother one of the nicest women on earth. There was a streak in Jesse that caused him to run wild. If we ever got into trouble, you could bet that Jesse was our leader. "Jesse's guardian angel never gets a moment's rest," my mother often remarked.

"And when Michael's around him, his own angel is pulling its hair out," my father would add. "I suppose he's behind most every thing those boys get into." Still, my father was fond of Jesse. He always recognized and appreciated a great imagination, and Jesse was very imaginative. Who else would have thought of releasing the skunk in the high school in order to have classes canceled? Trouble was, everyone knew that Jesse was the only one who could have thought up such a plan. The dead giveaway, though, was the smell that permeated both he and Seth New because the skunk did not wish to cooperate with the scheme.

It was Mickey who threw the first girl-boy party any of us ever attended. "You're whipped," Jesse complained and the rest of us agreed. After all, we faced the horror of Mickey walking Sandy Higgs home from school. We saw how they smiled at each other during Sunday school. They even held hands. Mickey thought we couldn't see, but the hideousness nearly blinded us.

We attempted to shame Mickey for weeks, tried to convince him that girls were the enemy and that camping on one of the barrier islands would be much more fun. We didn't need girls. Girls didn't like to cut bait or to fish. They squealed at the suggestion of playing Blind Man's Bluff. They didn't know how to light a good fire and build a sturdy fort. Devil Key was our choice for camping just because the name sounded evil, and ghost stories would hold much more clout if told there rather than its sister key. "We do that every weekend," Mickey never wavered in his conviction that it was time we all grow up. It didn't matter to us that he was right. We liked the carefree life, and letting girls inside the circle was unthinkable.

"She's a red-headed bean pole," I shamelessly attacked, hoping to open Mickey's eyes to the truth. "Her hair looks like that wire thing my mom uses to scrub the pots and pans." Not one of us realized how serious Mickey was toward Sandy. While the rest of us saw a Cinderella with ashes on her face, Mickey saw a future princess and what a priceless gem she would be.

Mickey's party was a set up from the start. We never noticed it coming. It did not occur to us that boy-girl parties meant we had to spend time with THEM! We naturally assumed THEY would have one side of the room and we the other. Mickey betrayed us in the worst way. We found we were targets of the opposite sex. It wasn't enough that he put his very best friends in this predicament, but he had involved our younger peers, boys that looked up to us. They were much more innocent. They should not have been victims of the terrible crime committed by our own Benedict Arnold. Poor Noah McGowan, a year younger and equally as naive, invited his best friend, Curt Davis. To make matters worse, Mrs. Roberts had been enlisted in this treasonous act. No matter how far we separated ourselves from the "things" in dresses, Sabrina Roberts drew us back together. We realized pretty quickly that each girl had a particular boy in mind, and we were to have no choice in the matter. Mickey had chosen his girl-friend, Sandy Higgs, but his victims were to have no say in this fiendish, terrible scheme. Each girl had her own particular move, and we were powerless to react. I watched as one by one each girl zeroed in on her "man." India Thompson nabbed Jesse; Sandy's younger sister, Blanchie, captured Noah; Bella McGowan snatched Curt Davis, and Seth, his girl was the slyest of all. Hannah Miller stood staring at him with sad, shy blue eyes, purposely aloof until Seth, filled with compassion, approached and signed to her, indicating in the language of the deaf that he would dance with her. Seth and Hannah's friend-ship went far beyond the understanding of the rest of us. He was the one that bonded with her after Scarlet Fever left her deaf at age eight. The bond was probably made stronger by the fact that her mother and his father remained close friends after Hannah's father left town and Seth's mother died. Despite the boy/girl barrier, Seth patiently learned her language while the rest of us struggled to communicate with her, but Hannah never laughed at us or made us feel foolish in our attempts to use the language she and Seth shared so well. She was infi-nitely patient with each of us. It was Seth that railed when he believed Hannah was left out of anything.

Seth's departure left me with the most hideous of all creatures. There were girls and there were pests, rodents, insects, and the most dreaded of all, "baby sisters." I was strangled as she dragged me to the makeshift dance floor. Her name was Valley Roberts. She was Mickey's less than charming sibling, and in order to save my friendship with Mickey, I took the first chance I could and ran all the way home where my father roared in laughter and my mother scolded me for my lapse in manners.

Childhood went quickly and before I knew it high school days were over. The autumn of my eighteenth year found me away at a small col-lege in Virginia. I always intended to leave home for school. I recog-nized this as the first step in the process of breaking away. Still, my adventurous spirit never wanted me to place such a distance between my mother and her home cooking. It was my lack of diligence in high school that dictated that I go to school where they would accept me, not where I wanted. Mickey Roberts remained close to home attending a local but prestigious university not more than a four-hour drive from the island. He was all-scholarship material, and this allowed him to make his own choice of schools. Sandy Higgs definitely grew into princess material, and she and Mickey planned to marry after his entrance into law school. Seth attended a junior college on the mainland while Jesse married Blanchie Higgs right out of high school. He worked in the local garage and did some general labor around town while harboring dreams of selling his first novel at an astronomical price and retiring into obscurity.

In all my life, I could not remember missing a Sunday morning at the Serenity Key Baptist Church. Neither Claire nor Trevor Abernathy would allow it. It wasn't that it was a duty. It was their joy not only to attend but also to assure that I gained the correct teaching. From the very start, I took my salvation for granted. I knew I was saved. The Bible told me it was a gift. A gift was free for the taking. I had to do nothing in return. I went to church and that should have told God I appreciated what he did for me. Right? While away at college, I slept late every Sunday, and studied late every Sunday night. I was free from the drudgery of church, from the burden of Christianity. My parents must have known my wayward acts, but except in passing they said nothing.

I did keep close tabs on my friends while I was away. I was surprised that I was the only one who truly wanted to leave space between Serenity and my choice of higher education. After two years of junior college and strenuous training, Seth New became Serenity's first paid fire chief. He would direct the all-volunteer force. "It will be only a matter of time," Mickey wrote to me, "before Hannah's blue eyes convince Seth it's time to marry." He also told me that he worried about Jesse. "He's never grown up, Michael. I talk to him, but he doesn't understand that leaving Blanchie home alone every night isn't responsible. He tells me that I'm just as whipped by Sandy as ever. He's drinking and gambling, and I think there are other women. I told him that Blanchie's going to divorce him if he keeps it up, but it's just a joke to him." They were soon to be in-laws, and I did not envy Mickey his challenge.

As time passed, I grew to enjoy life away from Serenity. I still missed my mother's home cooking, but I worked diligently so that my parent's hard-earned money was not wasted. I cut my teeth on the school's newspaper, and I clerked in the small town *Gazette*. As graduation neared, I found I relished life away from the island. I dreaded the thought of returning home permanently. I needed a reason to stay away. It wasn't that I didn't miss my parents or love them with all my heart, it was just that I knew they would always be there waiting for me while I went in search of the adventure that I craved.

Writing for my father's paper lacked the excitement I wanted to experience. For that reason, I prepared my resume' and mailed out copies to practically every newspaper in America. I knew that at least one publisher in one large city would see my talent and save me from the endless drudgery of articles regarding the small town little league, the town council's agenda, and visiting relatives.

Faith and hope, they are brothers destined for greatness. Cynicism and hopelessness, they are hapless friends on the road to ruin. That thought comes to me from time to time. I pondered its meaning while sitting beside my father, fresh from college, dressed in my black suit, listening to Jesse's father, Melvin Crum, tell all he knew about my momma as she laid before us in a closed casket. The pastor expounded her goodness, praised her love for others and thanked God that we could all rejoice in her salvation and the very fact that she was in Heaven and not before us dead and lifeless. It was there beside the man that I never knew to shed a tear that I received my first taste of utter devastation. I could not fathom that God who proclaimed his love for us would take our joy away. As my father bent forward attempting to control his emotions, his body heaving forth powerful sobs, I tried to console him, but I had nothing within me. There was only a vast emptiness, and at times I wasn't even sure that my heart was remembering to beat.

I was lost without my mother, and more than ever I wondered how Seth New survived without such a woman in his life. I could not eat, but I could sleep and that was the best way I knew to forget my loss. I received responses to my resume' in surprising number. Only a few days before my dreams had been on the verge of coming true. Now, I simply declined the offers and slipped the letters into the trash before my father could see them. There was absolutely no use to dream of a life beyond my reach. I could not leave Trevor Abernathy alone, not so soon after losing the one woman in our lives that meant everything to both of us.

Mickey returned home from school often to see his fiancé and prepare for their upcoming wedding. Without fail, he set aside time to spend with me. Even when I resisted his company, he would sit in silence until he felt he had worn out his visit. Then, he would leave always promising to return soon. He always kept that promise.

Seth would stop by on occasion, but he fumbled for words, and we both found the situation awkward. He would leave quickly, but like Mickey, he would return. I knew he cared, and I did appreciate his effort, but it was Jesse who worked the magic I needed. He could make me laugh when it was the last intention I held. He was a born clown, and some of Sabrina Roberts' storytelling skills had rubbed off on him. I never determined if it was a comedy routine or an act of great clumsiness, but I always laugh when I recall the day he slipped off my small sailboat and fell into the Gulf waters. Still, I know he never planned for the crab to latch on to his bare foot and hold on for dear life.

It was some time before I realized that cynicism and hopelessness were hitting the road and even if faith and hope remained elusive, I could still move on with my life. It was my father that brought me back again. As I began to watch him carefully his spirit began to renew itself. I wondered at the change that I saw occurring. "Back to work, Michael," he pulled the covers from me as I slept. "We have a business to run. Your momma wouldn't approve of us avoiding it one more day."

"Momma's not here, Dad," I rolled over pulling the sheet over my head as I did.

"She is, Michael," he sat on my bed. "She's all around us."

Slowly I lowered the covers thinking he must have gone mad and that was actually the change I saw in him. "What?"

"I walk past that cabinet with the collection of those silly salt and pepper shakers and I think of the joy she received when Millie at the antique store found her just the perfect pair.

"There's the afghan she crocheted two summers ago. She would sit with me in the evenings silently working on it while I prepared a story. She'd throw words to me because she knew better than me what was going on around here." I remember vividly that at that point he swallowed a large lump in his throat, and I thought I would see Trevor Abernathy cry once again. "But," his voice cracked under the strain of lifting his words from his heart to his mouth, "it's in you that I see her the most."

I felt my utter devastation melt away like ice on a hot day. I reached for my father. I was a grown man needing the comfort reserved for a child. My father cradled me while I released the grief and pain I held over the loss of the woman I loved most in the world. I suddenly understood my father's change. It occurred because he came to realize that Claire Abernathy was not completely gone from our lives. I knew there were memories of my mother that would always cause my heart to rise.

Life became livable again. I substituted joy with hard work. I printed detailed stories of every day life in the small island town. I covered the little league play offs. I sat in on the town council meetings, and I talked with the visiting relatives. It was a weekly paper and news, real news, was not a part of my father's *Serenade*. It was his stubborn opinion that a local paper need not delve into life in the outside world. "When it is your paper," he would point to me, "you can do whatever you like." I never expressed my intention of selling his paper when it became mine.

It was six months before the real feelings of restlessness set in, and they were quickly becoming something I could not hide. I was ready to move on. I convinced myself Dad could easily do the work. I held no doubt that it was really a one-man operation. Besides, he had Georgie to help him. Georgie was a part of Serenity Key as much as the waters that surrounded the island. When I attended high school, Georgie had been a grown man, but to everyone Georgie's mental retardation made him an eternal teenager. Since I could remember, he lived in his small cottage not far from my home or the *Serenade* office. He was able to care for himself by working odd jobs for just about every person in town. Without a doubt, everyone on the island considered Georgie part of his or her responsibility, but Georgie knew it was the other way around. His purpose in life was to assist others. His mind did not work at optimum level, but his heart made up the difference. Georgie loved everyone and everyone loved him. Dad told me often that Georgie had been a big help to him while I was away at college, and I saw no reason why the man-child couldn't continue to assist him once I left.

It was my intention to leave town, and I was going to tell my father. I wanted to tackle the world. I felt like a super hero about to be loosed on the unsuspecting public. Nothing could stop me. Nothing but a pair of celestial blue eyes in the shape of dew drops that hid behind wispy curls of auburn that fell about the face of an angel. Her name was Valencia, but she despised the name. It was her brother who provided the acceptable nickname of Valley. Mickey's sister smiled at me despite the fact that I practically knocked her over as I left Barney's Pharmacy. Suddenly the friendship I tried to save at age fourteen by fleeing Valley's grip as fast as possible seemed unimportant. "I'm —- I'm sorry." I apologized.

Her eyes danced. "It's okay, Michael. I'm used to your running away."

Those words could have been "I love you, Michael" for all my heart knew. It pounded hard against my chest. "Ho —- How are you, Valley?"

The thundering in my ears was so loud that I barely heard her answer. I silently cursed Mickey for not warning me of the peril I was in, the danger of losing my heart. "I was so sorry to hear about your mother. Sandy wrote me." I could only nod. I wondered where she had been, but I was unable to speak. It was impossible to gather my swirling thoughts.

"My momma's been a little sick lately. She's having some tests. I came home for awhile to be with her."

My mind took control of my emotions. "I hope things will be okay." I knew from Mickey that they suspected cancer, and the outlook was grim. Mickey continued in law school while his new bride cared for his widowed mother. Valley nodded, and I was struck by the immense sadness that suddenly appeared in her blue eyes. "Are you okay?"

"I was going to ask you the same," she touched my arm with her slender fingers, and I knew without a doubt that I would not be leaving Serenity Key in the near future.

"I'm doing okay."

"Well, Mr. Abernathy, I need to pick up Momma's medication," she opened the door to the pharmacy. "I'll probably see you around."

"Valley?" My throat tightened like a schoolboy's with a terrible crush. She stood waiting, but I was unable to speak.

"I'd love to," she winked. "When will you pick me up?"

"7:00," I croaked

"You won't run away this time?"

My cheeks burned as the color of my face turned a dark pink. "I promise."

"I'll be ready," she let the door close, and I was left to float toward the office.

Valley was the glue that held me to Serenity Key. I saw her daily. I found excuses to visit. I was a man who would have abandoned his entire set of dreams and ambitions for the complete love I craved from her. Valley, though, at times, seemed distant, almost restless.

It was cancer that the doctors found, and Sabrina Roberts was valiantly fighting. She refused to give up. My mother, I knew, would have faced such a disease in much the same way, but she had not been given the chance. The aneurysm had taken her quickly, too quickly. I watched with Valley as her mother lost her hair, her appetite, and her strength. Valley never seemed to want to spend time alone with Sabrina. "I can't, Michael. I just can't stand to sit in there one more day," she complained. "I'm afraid. I hate to see her like this."

"It makes her happy," I spoke softly to her. She needed comforting as much as her mother. "I'll sit with you." I made the time to spend with both of them. I watched the woman I loved struggle with the fear of loss. I held her when she cried. I declared my love and my protection, and in one day, she shunned them all.

Valley never indicated her intention of leaving. She just left. Her mother was devastated by her departure, and her brother was angry. I never knew Mickey to lose his composure, but on the day Valley departed, he was a lion unleashed. He paced back and forth in his living room cursing his sister. He swore that he would never forgive her for abandoning their mother when she needed her most.

"Aren't you being a little unfair? She needed a break. She'll be back in a day or two more refreshed. Your mother's cancer is in remission. The doctor's reports have been good. She probably thought this would be a good time to get away." I was ever Valley's protector.

My friend's mouth parted in disbelief. "She didn't even tell you, did she?" His words brought the bitterness he felt deep inside out into the open.

"No, she didn't tell me she was leaving. I understand, though."

"What do you understand?" He paced away from me but suddenly he turned, his eyes boring into my soul. "It can't be that she ran off with Brad Rasneck. She's not coming back, Michael. She's going to marry him. Where did you think she had been? I had to threaten her life to get her back here for Momma. If you had asked me, I would have told you to stay away from her, but you didn't."

"If you knew, I shouldn't have to ask. You should have told me." My head was pounding from the rejection that my heart was feeling.

"I thought there might be hope that she could find real happiness with you," Mickey offered a ready excuse.

His words were strung like a tight wire hanging from his mouth to my ear. There was a roar of unbelievable proportions as I blinked and coughed. "But you knew —— You suspected she was in love with Brad? You knew what she meant to me. I was playing second fiddle the entire time thinking I had a chance." I sat in the nearest chair almost missing the seat and landing on the floor. My heart began speaking. Denial hit me like a wave washing upon a sandy beach. "You're wrong," I told him. "I love her. I told her so. If there had been someone else she would have told me."

Mickey looked to where his bride entered the room. Sandy Roberts scolded us for trying to wake her sleeping mother-in-law. "He didn't know," Mickey's voice held more concern now than anger. "She never told him."

Sandy's look of pity was more than I could bear. I pushed myself up, made myself stand. "More importantly, Mick, you didn't tell me," I shook my head. "And I thought all along you were my best friend." I walked from their house. I felt no real anger toward Mickey or his sister. All I knew was that my heart was hardening, and there was a crack running straight down the middle. I wondered if Valley found my declarations of love simply amusing or down right laughable. I realized I had been more intelligent at fourteen. Whenever Valley Roberts was involved, running was the only option.

Serenity Key and its local paper became my prison. It would have been less of a punishment to be strapped to the electric chair with the current surging. Instead of a quick death, I was slowly being smothered. I worked hard so that at night I could simply fall into my bed too exhausted to dream. I left no time for thoughts of Valley. My intense love for her soured in her abandonment. I found myself wishing I could hate her. Then maybe the wound would heal. Instead, my love remained. It was just bitter in my soul. I found myself avoiding Valley's brother. I knew that one simple apology for my cruel words would have ended the strain between us, but somehow harboring the ill feelings worked like a narcotic to dull the pain Valley inflicted.

My father seemed clueless over my unhappiness. He never mentioned Valley's sudden departure, and I wondered if he ever really knew what I felt for her. Surely, I never told him the truth. It seemed he was content to have me working with him, knowing that someday I would take over where he left off. I could not have been more surprised when he confronted me.

Exhausted beyond belief I headed toward my room leaving supper on the table untouched. "Michael," he pushed his chair back and stood. I stopped in the doorway to my room, stepped back to where I could see him. "What is it?" He demanded.

"I'm tired, Dad." I felt my shoulders tense as if someone added another weight to the pound of stress already there. I knew it was my chance to tell him, but I could not bring myself to hurt him. I had allowed the charade to go on too long.

That he understood all too well became evident. "Of what?"

I shook my head. "Just tired, that's all."

He did not move. "Let's get it out. I'm tired, too. I'm tired of watching you struggle."

"I'm not struggling," I protested with a lie.

"Life shouldn't be hard, and it's only made that way by unhappiness." It was my mother's adage, however, coming from the strong tower of a man, it seemed more profound. "What's making it unbearable for you?" He asked.

"Dad, I'm a little too tired...."

"So!" His fist hit the dinner table causing the dishes to rise and fall with a clamor. Food fell from my untouched plate to the table. His glass of water spilled. Trevor seemed not to notice, but my eyes watched the water drip, drip, drip to the floor. "Let's get to the source of your lack of energy."

"All right!" I felt the bonds that kept my reserve intact stretch and then break coming back on me like a rubber band pulled too far. I lifted my eyes to face him. "I want life to be an adventure that I can't experience here. I want to write about real life, not some still-life picture in Serenity Key. Even the name of our town is boring. Dad, I can't understand why you left Detroit for this place. I lived more in the four years at college than I have all the others on this island! I hate it here! I don't want to be here." He looked as if I struck him, and I felt immediate remorse. I ran a hand through my hair. "I'm sorry," I cleared my throat and said the apology again so that he was sure to hear it.

He recovered, forced his lips into a turn that resembled a smile. "I asked you, didn't I?"

"But you didn't deserve it."

"Thank you for acknowledging that," he pulled a chair out and motioned that I should sit. When I did, he sat across from me. The silence stretched on unbearably as he searched for words I realized only much later were very difficult for him. "You and I have a difference of opinion separating us. You seem to believe that life cannot be experienced here. I believe that my life has been a wonderful experience. Adventure, Michael, is where you find it and what you do with it. Even town meetings can offer an excursion if you read between the lines and pull the real meat out of it." I started to speak, but he stopped me. "You want to discover life outside our fair island, and I want you to know that your happiness is important to me." For the first time, I noticed the folder beside him on the table. He opened it and lifted a set of papers. I sat dumbfounded as I leafed through a resume' package which included his personal recommendation, references from my college professors, and copies of my best work for the *Serenade* and the college paper where I also cut my teeth. Trevor Abernathy stood once again. His hand rested on my shoulder. "Go forth and experience your adventure, but come and look in on your old man from time to time." He stared at me for a long moment while my eyes rested on the documents, my passport to Paradise. "This island is as close to Heaven as you'll find on this Earth. It's not a perfect place, but you've never really experienced the world beyond." He closed the folder. "I love you. All your mother and I ever wanted for you, Michael, is to be happy." Picking up the package, he handed it across the table to me.

I realized that I could have returned the resume' and its attachments. I could have set them aside and never looked at them again. I knew that nothing would have made my father happier, but the open door of my prison was too much of an enticement. I walked through it, and I did not look behind me for a very long time.

Chapter Two

Round Trip Ticket

"And he arose, and came to his father. But when he was yet a great way off, his father saw him, and had compassion, and ran and fell on his neck, and kissed him." - Luke 15:20

I would like to say that I chose a busy metropolitan area in which to venture, but actually, it chose me. If the truth were known, I believe my father pulled the strings that allowed me to work for the same paper he left so many years before. My boss was a crusty old journalist who relinquished his writing pencil for a promotion to editor. He had known my father well, and that fact only strengthened my conviction that it was whom my father knew and not what I knew that had gotten me the job.

I was provided a desk inside a cubicle, but there was never time to enjoy my piece of real estate in the busy office. If there was a fire, I was called to cover it. If there was a murder, I was the man who wrote the lurid details. I covered the juicy trials, and the stories of missing children. I cornered the victims. I interviewed the killers. I made sure the photographers captured images that showed the sorrow in every incident. I never once attended a town council meeting or interviewed the chairman of the latest festival happening in Detroit. Not once did I have a picture taken of the catch of the day held by a five-year old boy or report on the 50th anniversary of a much beloved couple.

Coming from Serenity Key where everyone knew the most intimate details of my life to an area where no one cared took some adjustment.

I struggled with loneliness, but after the first year of working almost non-stop, I found my attitude as guarded as the locals. There was not a day that I didn't walk past homeless men, women and children or watch an ambulance pull away with an injured or dead victim inside. The first suicide I actually viewed, unable to stop, stung a bit, but by the third or fourth, I did not even blink. I wrote about it all without remorse and made sure the most graphic of pictures was taken. Everyday I woke expecting more to come. If it didn't I rationalized I would be out of business. My social life was non-existent. I did not have close friends nor did I have time to make any.

I received one letter from Mickey almost a year after my move to Detroit. He stated that he had a little under a year to go before graduating law school. "Momma's cancer is still in remission," he advised. "She hasn't really recovered her strength. She gets out a little more lately, but Sandy is still at home to help her. You know, Michael, I've never heard my wife complain one time. Momma loves her like her own." There was more there to say, and I was thankful he didn't mention the absence of his sister. After all, it was Valley's place to be home with her mother, to help Sandy. He also reported that Seth had married. "Hannah's taking it real hard," he wrote. "She's been his best friend for all these years, and he meets and falls in love with Linda almost over night. Linda's a wonderful girl, though, and Hannah will warm up to her. I guess for Seth, it was love at first sight."

I laughed bitterly. No one knows better than Michael Abernathy love at first sight is a farce.

"Jesse still hasn't wised up, and I know that divorce is just around the corner. I can't understand how Blanchie can put up with his cheating let alone his gambling and drinking." I knew that if you loved someone, you could put up with just about anything except their leaving you behind. "Our old buddy, Curt Davis, was elected Chief of Police. He and his officer are stirring things up. Now, there's some real news." He ended the letter without a clue as to what Curt was doing that caused a commotion in the sleepy little town. "Write back, okay?" He asked. When I finished reading the letter I folded it up, placed it back into the envelope and never answered it. It was the first and last correspondence Mickey sent, and each time I looked in the drawer where I placed it and saw it lying there, I felt a pang of guilt at not having met my old friend half way.

Christmas came and went for a second year. There was no time to return home. My father had to be content with my gift, my card and my call. The third Thanksgiving found me at my desk working on a piece that covered a gang's infiltration of a local neighborhood. "What are you doing here?" The voice was a familiar one. I looked up to see the crusty old journalist leaning over the wall of my cubicle. He smelled of the very best in bourbon.

"Hey, Ted," I stopped pounding on the keyboard and turned to face him. "Better yet, what are you doing here?"

"My wife's mother. I only see her twice a year, and that's too much," he grumbled and reached across the aisle from me to retrieve a chair. "Your father all alone this year?"

He was playing my guilt like the strings on a harp. "Yeah, but he understands," I told him.

"I'm sure he does, but that doesn't make it right, does it?"

I studied him for a long moment. Was he trying to deliver a message? "Did he call you?"

Ted shook his head. "Your father and I were tight way back when. That was before he left. We shared letters every once in a while, but I figure he just wanted to forget about the *Ledger* and Detroit. I was real surprised when he phoned me and told me you were looking for a job. I would have thought he would try to keep you as far away from here as possible."

"Why's that?" I leaned back in my chair, stretched, laced my fingers and placed my hands behind my head. Ted looked at me through thick glasses that made his eyes seem a bit larger than normal.

"You can ask me that?" He shook his head.

"Did something happen here, Ted? Was my father fired?"

"Fired?" Behind the glasses, his eyes widened in surprised then narrowed. "How old were you when your father moved you to wherever it is you're from?"

I thought he should remember, but I answered him anyway. "I'm from Serenity. Dad and Mom moved there before I was born."

"You never knew your Uncle Carl, then. I thought he was a nice guy. He had problems. We all had problems. Some of us just deal with them better than others. He didn't deal with his well at all."

"My father had a brother?"

Ted stood. "I thought you knew about it. I'm telling you, Michael, I was wondering from the start how you could hurt your father by coming to the one town he vowed never to set foot in again, but you never even knew what drove him out of here. I know he worries about you, you being his only son and all."

"Ted," I was confused. "You're talking in circles. Let's bring it down to the main idea." I used the same words Trevor Abernathy hammered into my brain when I rambled on with my writing unable to quite bring my ideas under control.

Ted walked away from me without a word. I wanted to follow him, but I didn't want to appear to be a puppy after a bone. My mind was swirling. Ted was mistaken. My father would have told me about a brother, an uncle, if he existed. I shook the thought away and sat slowly in my chair. I continued to work on my story. When the phone rang I answered it, listened, gave a nod that the caller could not hear and hung up the phone. I saved the material I had typed into the computer and jumped up to grab my coat. I fell right against Ted, knocking him back a step or two. "Sorry," I mumbled. "I have to go. There's been a gang shooting. It's a great addition to my piece."

Ted held out a paper, yellowed by time, and I took it. "When you have the opportunity read this," he told me. "It'll answer all your questions, and we never have to let Trevor know I spilled the beans."

"Sure," I tucked the paper into my coat pocket. "Thanks, Ted. Go home and enjoy your family." I rushed out the door and into the cold streets of a town I had stopped pretending to like.

In the emergency room of the local hospital, I brushed snow off my coat sleeves as I waited to obtain news about the victims of a gang shooting. The information clerk confirmed that my source had not sent me on a wild goose chase.

The lobby was packed with sick men, women and children. The area was not a wealthy one, and the children's clothing was threadbare and not heavy enough for the season. Old women moaned and grown men coughed. I took it all in. Talking with Ted about my father made me somewhat homesick. I thought about Serenity. It wasn't a perfect place, but there was not one person who, if they saw a child without proper clothing, would not find a way to provide a coat, a sweater, or a pair of shoes. There was not an elderly person on the island that did not have, at the very least, one warm, delicious meal a day. It was that thought that made me blink twice as I scanned the room. I rubbed my eyes. I knew that it could not be so, but there in the midst of the madness in the lobby sat a thin woman with auburn hair streaming down her shoulders and tears falling from her blue eyes that were dark and puffy. Her lip was cut, and she held a makeshift bag of ice against it. I blinked again wondering why a memory I long buried would haunt me now.

Opening my eyes, the vision did not vanish. Slowly, I walked toward the woman. She looked up. Her lips parted in surprise and immediately she tried to hide her injuries with her hands. "Valley?" I whispered her name.

"Go away, Michael," she refused to look at me. "Please just leave."

"You know I can't do that. What happened to you? Were you in an accident? Is Brad here with you?"

She lowered her hands, but her eyes never looked into mine. "Yes. Yes, that's what it was."

"You're lying," the lady beside her shook her head. She was older by a few years. Her voice carried the rasp of a heavy smoker. Her grayish hair was tied into a scarf. "Her old man did this, but what's new? They expect her in here once a week."

"Please, Corrine," Valley begged.

"If I thought it would do any good, I'd tell him what you've been through, but it wouldn't make a difference so I'm going outside to have a smoke." She stood slowly and shuffled away.

"Is that true?" I took the seat the woman vacated. Valley would not answer. "Did Brad do this to you?" I demanded.

She nodded her head, and for the first time, I noticed the dullness in the once shining locks. Her skin held tiny cracks that revealed its dryness. Her coat was too thin for the weather outside, and her clothes were obviously bought second hand. Her shoes were almost worn through. "Where is he?" Anger warmed my blood. It was all I could do to keep my voice below a roar. "I'll kill him."

"No," she clutched at me as I started to stand. "No," she sobbed. "He's at the jail. He'll sleep there tonight. Tomorrow it will be all right. He'll be fine."

"All right?" I stared at her in disbelief. "It's not okay. Your friend said he does this all the time."

"She exaggerates."

"It doesn't matter. To do this to you one time is — It's —- I'll kill him! Why do you stay? You have family."

"I have no family," she sighed. "I walked out on them. Don't you remember? I walked out on you, too. Get away from me, Michael."

"Mickey is still your brother, and I'm — I'm still a friend, Valley."

"That's the past."

"Maybe for you, Valley, but I don't walk out on friends when they need me."

She laughed bitterly, "You just run."

Had I hurt her so badly or was she just trying to hurt me? I never realized that a silly fourteen-year old boy's slight of etiquette would cause her to feel the way she did so many years later. "Valley, if that ever bothered you, why didn't you tell me? I would have told you how stupid I had been. Didn't you realize that I loved you? I told you I did."

"It doesn't matter, Michael."

"It does," I tried to reach for her hand, but she pulled back from me.

"I love Brad," she whispered. "This is my fault. I make him mad. I should know better."

"What could you have done to deserve his hands ever touching you in any other way but tenderness and love?"

"Don't you see, he doesn't know any other way?"

I heard the story so many times, the wife blaming herself for her husband's brutality. I had come to accept the insane attitude from other women, but I could not accept it from Valley. Mickey, Sr., and Sabrina provided Valley with a loving home. Her mother and father respected each other, and their children were cherished. She lost her father young, but she knew him. She could not have forgotten the love he showed to her and to her brother. "He has no right. He's sick. You need to get away from him. I'll put you on a plane back home tonight. I'll go with you if you need me."

"I don't need you!" She screamed at me. "I can't leave Brad!" Her voice was laced with panic.

"Mrs. Rasneck," the nurse called her name. I could do nothing. I knew that. I scribbled on a piece of paper from my notepad as she stood. Tearing it out, I shook it at her desperate to provide her with a lifeline. "Here's my number."

"I can't keep that," her eyes grew large. "If Brad found it, he'd be angry."

"Then you can —- I work at the *Ledger*. Can you remember that?"

"I know where you work, Michael." She pushed past me angrily and out of my life once again.

I pulled my coat around me as I stepped outside through the double doors that lead to the parking lot. I wasn't sure if the trembling of my body was due to the cold or from Valley's rejection of help. "Mister?" The woman I met inside stopped me. "You got to get her away from him. He's —- That man is a monster when he drinks, and lately, he's been drinking a lot. He lost his job about a month ago. He blames it all on her."

"I don't know what I can do?"

"You're Michael, aren't you?" Her stare went through my soul.

"I'm Michael," I confirmed.

"Then you're probably about the only one who could do anything for her. She won't listen to anyone. Her husband's been telling her no one cares about her. She's been told so many times that she's worthless that she believes it."

"So, what can I do to make her believe she's not worthless?"

"When she talks to me about you, Mister, her eyes shine. I think you're an ember in her soul that still has some spark to it."

"I think you're mistaken," I corrected. "Valley and Brad have been married for a long time."

"I'm not mistaken," the woman's slender fingers reached out and gripped the collar of my jacket. "And if you don't do anything, she's not going to make it. Brad gets closer and closer to killing her every time this happens."

I pulled free and reached in my jeans pocket. I pulled out the cash I had on hand and said a silent prayer of thanks to God that the long weekend caused me to withdraw much more than usual. "When she gets done here, use a little of this to buy her a good dinner, a hot meal.

You, get something, too. Tomorrow, take her to the store, and buy her some warm clothing."

"This is your solution?" She pushed the money back at me.

"No," I refused to take it back. "I can't stand to think of her in those threadbare clothes. There's something else you need to do."

The woman listened carefully to my every word. When I finished, she smiled. "You're a good man, just like she's always saying."

"You promise to do what I've asked? I can count on you?"

"You can count on Corrine," she nodded, and I walked away. In my line of work, I found so few human beings that cared. Corrine was an exception to the rule.

It was the first deadline I missed in my journalistic career. I left the hospital parking lot and went directly to the police station. I learned from the desk sergeant that Brad would be held until arraignment the next day at which time, if history held true, Valley would appear and plea for her husband's release. Brad would go home. He would be on his best behavior until the charges were dropped because Valley would not cooperate with the District Attorney. Then, possibly one day, one week, but certainly no longer, Brad would be an overnight visitor once again, and the cycle would repeat.

I had not worked for the *Ledger* without gaining contacts in the various governmental offices. The desk sergeant provided me with the name of the unlucky District Attorney who would attend arraignments the next day for those arrested over Thanksgiving. I thought about seeing Brad Rasneck while he sat behind bars, but so vivid was the picture of the fear on Valley's face when I offered my number that I knew it would definitely cause her harm.

My next stop was the home of the Assistant District Attorney. He was very gracious although I interrupted his Thanksgiving evening. I provided him with the information I gleaned from Corrine and from the police department. I told him what I knew of Valley and her husband. The questions that he asked assured me that he was taking Valley's plight seriously. Before I left him, he promised every effort to keep Brad Rasneck behind bars, and I assured him that I would contact her family. "Women like your friend need counseling," he advised. "I'll do everything I can to force him into a guilty plea. If he pleads guilty, I'll ask the friend, Corrine, to testify to the serious nature of the beatings. If he pleads innocent, I'll request that he be given a high bond. Corrine's testimony could help there, too. I'll pull his record for the Court. There shouldn't be any problem." I understood his reasoning. If Valley's husband realized that he would remain behind bars should he plea innocent, it was possible that he would enter a guilty plea to the misdemeanor charge, thus providing the attorney for the state the opportunity to request misdemeanor probation to include a condition of counseling. If Corrine appeared in Court with Valley, she would contradict any assertions by Valley that everything was fine. She could describe Brad's continued violence and Valley's current mental state. It might even assure jail time for Brad. A violation of probation would also be helpful in deterring any violent reactions from Brad toward Valley. Probation would keep him on a tight leash, and the next arrest for spouse abuse would come with a charge of violation of probation attached.

Leaving the attorney's home, I walked the streets. The snow had stopped falling, and for the first time I took a moment to realize my prospects for the following day. The town would be dirty, dingy and filled with crime. It would continue to be that way for a long time. I wondered about the adventure I had been seeking when I left Serenity Key. When did I stop wanting to experience life? Why had I settled so easily for the morbid side of humanity?

When I reached my apartment, I immediately dialed the number that I phoned so many times in my youth. The call woke Mickey. Without an apology or polite chatter, I told him about my meeting with his sister. I made him aware in no uncertain terms that Valley needed him in Detroit.

"How can I find her?" He asked. "Did she give you her address, a phone number?"

"I didn't get her address, and I doubt she even has a phone. She'll be in the courtroom tomorrow morning when Brad's arraigned. I've spoken to the Assistant D.A., and he knows the situation."

There was an awkward moment of silence until he spoke to me again. "This has happened more than once, and she keeps going back to him?"

"According to the friend that brought her to the emergency room, it's an ongoing scenario, and it's getting worse every time."

"Why, Michael?" His voice was strained. "Why didn't she just call me?"

"She feels alienated from you. According to her friend, Brad's put a lot of doubt in her head. He's a typical abuser. He separates her from those she loves by filling her with lies. He tells her you don't love her. He makes her believe that you hold it against her because she left you. He tells her that you never want to see her again."

"But why would she believe him?"

"I don't think it's something we can understand unless we go through it. A lot of women I have interviewed tell me they feel like no one cares for them except their abuser. There's no way out of the endless cycle. One minute the man is loving and attentive. The next he's beating her, swearing at her, and he's telling her it's all her fault. Then, things settle down, and he's sorry, and he promises it will never happen again. Things are okay for a while. She stays, and then it begins again. The cycle is only broken when the abused party is either killed or walks away successfully."

"What do you mean, walks away successfully?" I heard the fear in his voice.

"A man who abuses his wife, very often doesn't want her to leave him, and sometimes he'll kill her to keep her from walking out on him."

"Momma can't know about this, Michael," his voice cracked with emotion. "Did she even ask about her?"

I wished I could lie, but I knew he deserved the truth. "No, Mick, but honestly, Valley was in a lot of pain, emotionally and physically. I was the last person on earth she wanted to see, at least at that moment."

"Momma's dying," Mickey spoke the words as if they were something he did not want to admit. "I hate to leave her. She might die while I'm gone."

"Your sister might die if you don't leave." My words were harsh but true. "Will you be on a plane?" There was between us a strain that stretched the miles. He was quiet for some time.

"I'd ask you to meet me, but I think there's something you should know."

"What?" I wondered what terrible thing he had done to separate us even further.

"It's Trevor," his voice was barely a whisper above the pounding of my heart.

⋆ ✝ ⋆

The news that my father was obviously not well shook me badly. I was a negligent son. I paid no attention to his needs, and he definitely needed me. I packed quickly, stopping at the *Ledger* to type a note that explained my need for emergency leave. After my earlier conversation with Ted, I knew he would understand.

It wasn't until I was on the plane that I remembered the paper that the crusty old fellow handed to me in the office. Removing my coat, I pulled it from the pocket. I settled into the seat and searched for what it was he intended me to see.

It was just a small byline written by another reporter, and the reason was made obvious by the photo. It was my father leaning over a gurney. A sheet covered the body that lay upon it. Trevor was obviously in distress and unable to hold his emotions. The headline read, "Man Kills Wife, Two Children before Turning Gun on Self." I looked at the picture more carefully. There was not one gurney, but four with sheets covering those bodies lying upon them. The picture moved me. It caught the essence of my father's grief. I stared at it for a long while before I read the article explaining that an uncle I never knew existed had murdered his family and turned the gun upon his self. It set out in matter-of-fact tones that my uncle had been under a lot of stress. He lost his job due to a lay off at the factory where he worked, and he had been notified that his home would be foreclosed. Other woes were described. His youngest child had needed medication he could not afford. His wife lost another child only days before, and even with all that information, there was one line, one quote from my father, that told me exactly what was behind his departure from the big city. "I shouldn't have been so busy chasing news that I didn't see the needs of my own family. Never again. Never again."

I folded the paper and held it in my hand. His words and the image of that photograph haunted me as the plane taxied down the runway.

I took a deep breath. I was going home. If only for a while, I was returning to the uncomplicated place of my birth. I was sure that during that early morning, the day after Thanksgiving, the jet that whisked me away from Detroit and the plane Mickey had taken passed in the darkness, both traveling to those who needed us the most.

Chapter Three

The Apperance Of Angels

"And I am persuaded, that neither death, nor life, nor angels, nor principalities, nor powers, nor things present, nor things to come, nor height nor depth, nor any other creature, shall be able to separate us from the love of God, which is in
Christ Jesus our Lord."
- Romans 8:38 and 39.

I arrived at the airport and flagged a taxi by 5:00 that morning. It was nice to discard my coat for the warmer climate. It was 6:30 when I opened the front door that in my entire lifetime remained unlocked. I placed my bag at the door and stepped softly through the house. It was dark at first, but light began to shine through the windows as the sun rose. I found my father asleep in the recliner with the television on so low it was almost unheard. "Dad?" Bending, I softly touched his arm.

He opened his eyes, blinked. His hand covered mine. "Michael?" To me, it seemed there were no changes to my father's features.

"Yes, Sir," I smiled. I could not remember ever being happier to see him. Mickey had indicated to me that his was a grave illness. I did not see that, at least not immediately.

"What are you doing here?" He struggled to sit straight as if it took every bit of strength. It was then that the age showed more in his actions than in the changes on his face, and I had to swallow hard before telling him the lie. "I'm back. My adventures led me back home. Am I welcome? Is there room for one more to work on your paper?"

Tears sprang into his eyes and washed away my guilt for telling him the lie I knew would make him happy. His hand moved to my face as if I were his small boy once again. "I prayed you'd find your way back home. You seemed so happy in Detroit."

"Well, it wasn't home, and it didn't have you," I stood. "I'll fix us some breakfast."

It took him a few moments, but he got to his feet and followed me into the kitchen. "I've got some grapefruit. I'm going to have one of those. The doctor has me on a very strict diet."

"For what?" I asked casually.

"It's nothing really. I just need to watch what I eat. I'm not a young man any more."

"Inside, Dad," I felt the urge to hug him to me. "Inside you are," I slipped my arms around him carefully and held him close. "I missed you very much."

"I missed you," his voice was deep with conviction. "It's been a long three years. We're going to have a wonderful Christmas, you and me together again."

At that moment I realized I would not be returning to my job at the *Ledger* for a very long while; and if they would not hold a position for me, I would possibly have to attempt to find my adventures elsewhere. I was not saddened by that possibility because I knew that the alternative was something I never wanted to face. In order to leave Serenity Key again, it would have to mean that my father no longer needed me, and in his condition, I knew that while he was alive, he would need me near.

I began to work immediately. I pretended not to notice that Dad was moving slower, tiring easily, and that he never ventured into the paper. I realized as soon as I entered the office and printing area that it had been unused for some time. Several months of weekly issues went unpublished. I thought about talking it over with him, but his youthfulness seemed to spring back as I worked, and I did not want to see the tiredness appear on his face again. I delivered the paper on its due date, the Wednesday after Thanksgiving, and I felt like I know a proud father must feel over the birth of a child. I received praise and congratulations from the regular readers who thought that Serenity had actually lost its one and only paper, and I realized for the first time that my father's life had been spent doing something that everyone appreciated.

My father met me at the door, the paper in his hand. "Great job. Great job."

I let the door close behind me, "I enjoyed doing it, Dad."

"Thank you for not bringing up the fact that the paper's been down," he moved through the house after me.

"Why didn't you tell me you stopped printing?" I questioned him casually moving into the kitchen for a drink.

"It's up now," he beamed.

"It would have never been down if you had called me. I would have come home."

"But it wouldn't have been your choice," his bent frame straightened, and I saw a flash of his old pride. "It had to be your choice."

I never loved him more that I loved him at that moment. He would have spent the remainder of his life in misery, watching his paper die, praying that I would return, rather than tell me the truth and have me return against my will. Still, my conscience exploded. Ted, at the *Ledger*, assured me an indefinite leave, but I knew I would be returning when I was no longer needed in Serenity. I would sell the paper and leave the small island far behind me. Trevor had been speaking, and I did not hear. "I'm sorry. What?"

"It was your choice?" He repeated.

"Yes. You know it was," I fumbled with the words. "Ha—- Have you eaten yet?"

"I had some of that low fat mush the doctor has me on," he nodded.

"I have a few errands on the mainland," I told him. "Would you like to get out?"

"I'm going to take a nap," he informed and started toward his bedroom. "It was a better job than I have ever done," the compliment was thrown over his shoulder.

"Excuse me?"

"The paper. You learned a lot in Michigan. I'm glad you had the opportunity to go."

I nodded, and as he closed his bedroom door, I hurried from the house. Even as a child, telling blatant falsehoods to my parents bothered me, and the burden of the lie I just told sat heavily on my shoulders. There was also the image in the paper, my father's agony on display for the entire world to see that pricked at my conscience. I felt like a child harboring an important secret. I knew it was important to talk to him, but it seemed the hardest thing to do.

I did not head out of town immediately. I pulled the old pick up in front of the Roberts' home. I told myself it would be the first chance to see my old friend. Work had buried me since my return, but Valley and her brother were never far from my thoughts. Sandy Roberts answered the door. She seemed weary and worn, but she had the energy to offer me a warm embrace. "Welcome home."

"Mickey back yet?" I looked beyond her into the house.

"He'll be in this afternoon with or without Valley," her voice became a whisper as she pushed the screen door open. "Momma's not doing well. I think she wants to leave us, Michael, but something's holding her here."

"Sandy, she's a fighter. She's been battling this thing for years. She's not going to just roll over for it, and let it have its way."

Sandy's eyes became moist, "I love her like my own mother, but it's been so hard. I don't understand why she struggles with death. Remember in Sunday school how she described Heaven, how someday she'd be there, and she expected everyone of us to join her?"

I remembered vividly, and I nodded. "You look tired. Is there anything I can do?"

"No. Momma's settled in."

"Is she asleep?"

Sandy shook her head.

"Let me go visit her, and you have a cup of tea or a nap."

She was thankful for the reprieve and led me upstairs where Sabrina Roberts lay in her hospital bed. Her bones were almost evident through her thin skin. She no longer resembled the vibrant woman I knew as a child, my Sunday school teacher, the woman God used to open my heart to His salvation, the person who lead me on adventures through the stories she read, one of my mother's best friends. "Mickey?" She could not see me clearly until I approached.

"No, Mrs. Roberts. Michael Abernathy," I greeted.

"Do you remember Michael?" Sandy stood beside me.

She nodded although I was not totally convinced she did. "I wanted to stop in and say hello," I sat in a chair by her bed.

"Thank you," her voice was hoarse. "I enjoy visitors."

"Well, I would have stopped by earlier, but I had a deadline to meet."

"The paper?" She proved she did recognize me.

"The *Serenade*," I smiled.

"Thank you, Lord," she said almost to herself, and I shared a puzzled glance with Sandy. Sabrina made a feeble motion by raising her arm and pointing with her hand. "The angel," she spoke to her attentive daughter-in-law.

Sandy smiled her understanding and reached over me. "Momma wants you to see this," she placed the item gingerly in my hands. It was a dainty ornament made from an art form that never ceased to amaze me even though I grew up watching my mother with shuttle and string make beautiful items seemingly from nothing. It was an angel tatted with light blue thread. On its simple head of wood, it wore a halo made of golden chenille wire. Attached to a string that rose from its head was a nicely written Bible verse. "For I am persuaded, that neither death, nor life, nor angels, nor principalities, nor powers, nor things present, nor things to come, nor heights, nor death, nor any other creature, shall be able to separate us from the love of God which is in Christ Jesus, our Lord. Romans 8: 38 and 39," I read aloud.

"Yes. Yes," Mrs. Roberts seemed to be soothed by the verse.

"It's her favorite," Sandy advised.

"What a wonderful gift." I could see where comfort could be received simply knowing that someone cared enough to think of you and provide you with an item of such simple beauty.

"Find them," Mrs. Roberts turned to me, her eyes pleaded, "I'd like to know."

"Find them?" I mouthed silently to Sandy.

"We don't know who left it, and Momma wants to thank the person. It's been here a month, but it never ceases to bring her great joy."

"Would you?" Sabrina Roberts asked again.

I held the angel by its string so that both of us, Sabrina and I, could behold its beauty. I thought at first that it had been a special gift given by my mother in times past. I was almost disappointed. "I could put a note in the paper," I sat the angel on the stand beside the bed.

"I'd like to thank them in person."

"She wants you to find the maker so she can thank them. She does not want to put her gratitude in the paper," Sandy placed a comforting hand over her mother-in-law's frail fingers.

"I'll try, Mrs. Roberts," I assured. "Right now, I'd like to visit with you for a few minutes. If Sandy has the paper, we could read."

She nodded, and Sandy left to retrieve the *Serenade* returning with it in hand. I met her at the door. "Go rest," I whispered. She hesitated only a moment then offering me a warm smile, she walked toward the back stairs that lead to the kitchen.

Mrs. Roberts and I spent a long while with the *Serenade*. I would read and embellish, and she would smile and nod. I wondered if anyone realized how starved she was for news of the outside world. If something peaked her interest we would go over it again and try to determine the real facts. I was reminded of my father's comments about council meetings being adventurous if you read between the lines and got to the meat of things.

After a long while of reading without a response, I looked up to see the woman asleep. I folded the paper quietly and stood. As I rose my eyes fell on the angel, and I was reminded of my promise to try to locate the artist. I read the verse silently and knew it must have offered comfort to Sabrina. It was from her that I learned well the meaning behind the death, burial and resurrection of Jesus Christ. I knew from her teaching that God never moved. He was a sovereign Lord, and as the verse explained, there was nothing I could do to have His love depart from me once He knocked on the door to my heart and opened it. He knocked once a very long time ago, and I obeyed. The memory of that day flooded in upon me. Sabrina had been teaching in Romans and taught us that we were sinners (something my father often taught me with a belt at that age), and that Jesus had died for our sins. Mickey and Jesse made their usual snide remarks, and for once, I ignored them, failing to join in their antics to annoy Mickey's mother. I listened intently, hanging on to every word. I said nothing throughout the class, but as my classmates left, I stayed behind. There, alone in the Sunday school room where I spent endless hours, Sabrina showed me that Jesus did love me. In fact, He loved me so much that if I had been the only one left on Earth, He would have died for me. At that moment, I wanted nothing more in the world then to know for sure that I was actually God's child and an heir to His kingdom. Together, on our knees, I prayed with Sabrina for Jesus' love to cover my sins. I never felt so much peace, so free from worry as I had at that moment.

"For I am persuaded that neither death, nor life, nor angels, nor principalities, nor powers, nor things present, nor things to come, nor heights, nor death, nor any other creature, shall be able to separate us from the love of God which is in Christ Jesus, our Lord." The words ran through my mind once again, and I felt their comfort. There was a peace in knowing that Jesus had opened the door to my heart as a child and that even my current lack of faith could not keep Him from me. I walked away from Him, but he was always near.

After my mother's death, my heart seemed so hardened against the Lord. I could not imagine why He would take her away from me and from my father when we both so obviously needed her. Standing in Sabrina's room, hearing only her breathing, I began to realize that I had been the selfish one. The way of my mother's passing had been God's gift to her. He saved her from all the pain and struggle that Sabrina was going through. She was in a much more pleasant afterlife with Jesus, and Sabrina would soon be with her there. I bent and kissed Sabrina's cheek tenderly. She did not move, and I walked quietly from her room and downstairs to the kitchen. Sandy was there at the breakfast nook, her hands warmed by the tea in her cup.

She looked up as I entered. "Thank you."

I advised her that Sabrina was sleeping.

She nodded, "Momma will understand if you can't find the person who gave her the angel."

"Did it just appear or what?" My curiosity was peaked.

Sandy nodded once again. "She had a few visitors the day I noticed it."

"Who? Do you recall?"

"I was busy. Georgie and I were doing some heavy work Momma wanted done. We were beating out some of the heavy rugs and airing out mattresses, stuff like that. I remembered thanking God for the visitors so that I could get to the work." She thought for a second. "Chief Davis stopped by."

"Chief Davis, Curt?"

"Yeah," she smiled. "We call him Chief. It's a joke. He absolutely hates the title."

"He's doing well?" I hoped, remembering Mickey's last letter and the mystery surrounding Curt's office.

"He's fine. He brought Lonnie Culver with him. They visited awhile, and then Noah McGowan and Bella Edwards stopped in."

I ran my hand through my hair that was desperately in need of a trim. "Well, out of that crowd, Bella, being a woman engaged to a recent seminary graduate would be the most obvious." The announcement of their engagement had appeared in the last paper that my father printed. They were to marry after Noah returned from seminary, and I wasn't sure why they had not yet held the ceremony.

"I thought about that," she sipped her tea. "But when I called Bella, she said it wasn't her."

"What about her Aunt Rosa?"

"I'm ahead of you there, too. Bella said that Rosa crochets, no tatting. Rosa told her that there were a few women who took lessons from your mother, but it was so long ago she couldn't give any names."

"We have the beginnings of a little mystery here, I think."

"It's not a little mystery," Sandy started to take a sip of tea but sat the cup down instead.

"No?" My eyebrows lifted. I felt a story building like a tornado, and I could see an adventure beginning to kick up in the wind.

"Several angels have shown up in town. They appear when someone needs some encouragement or hope or just a verse."

"Who else?" I felt like the news hound I thought I left back in Detroit.

"Well, Blanchie for one."

"Your sister?" I was surprised. "What could Blanche need with a tatted angel?"

"She and Jesse are divorcing," Sandy's voice was pained, and I knew that she loved Jesse almost as much as she loved her sister. I was not surprised by her revelation simply because Mickey's letter of so long ago had intimated such. "He seems bent on destroying every good thing in his life."

"Did Blanchie receive a Bible verse?" My memory failed to come up with a comforting verse on divorce.

"Ecclesiastes 3:1, 5 and 6."

"To everything there is a season and a time to every purpose under the heaven," the words to the first verse flew from my memory. The rest I could not recall.

"A time to cast away stones, and a time to gather stones together, a time to embrace, and a time to refrain from embracing. A time to get and a time to lose, a time to keep and a time to cast away," Sandy completed, and I remembered that she always won the Bible verse contests in Sunday school.

"I can't believe that anyone would try to tell your sister that divorce is the right thing to do."

"I don't think that's the meaning behind it at all. I think it confirmed a few things for Blanchie. You need to talk to her."

"Has anyone ever received the same verse?"

Sandy shrugged her shoulders. "I don't know."

I sat with her for a while, and I wrote down the names of all those who appeared the day the angel was found. "You said Georgie was around. For a man with the brain of a child, he doesn't miss much," I commented and Sandy did not reply. "Dad told me often when I called what a big help he's been, but I haven't seen him since I arrived."

"Jake New's been using him at the restaurant, some really big project." That explained it. Big projects took all of Georgie's attention. When the project was over, I'd be seeing him, and I was actually thankful. I could remember when I thought the paper a one-man operation. Either the work had grown harder or I was simply out of practice.

Sandy sipped her tea once again and looked out the window. "You didn't come by to see Mickey, did you?" She asked out of the blue. I fumbled with words until she turned and gave me a bright smile. "He misses you, though. He knew Valley had been with Brad for some time, but when she returned home, Mickey was hopeful that you would change her mind. You were around so much, I think he talked himself into believing that Valley decided to stay because of you." She reached across the table and taking my hand in hers, she brushed her thumb across it as if she were soothing the hurt of a ten-year old child. "The morning she left and he had to tell you, Michael, he was more upset for you than he was for any other reason."

I could only nod. I could not lie to her and tell her that my hurt had been resolved.

"What's a little anger between friends?" She coaxed. "Don't throw your friendship away because of Valley. Mickey will be the first to admit that his sister's not worth it, at least not right now."

I cleared my throat of the emotion I felt. It would show if I allowed it. "What do you think the angels mean?" The question seemed to have a life of its own. It floated from the back of my mind, and I recognized it right away as highly important.

Sandy thought for a long moment. "Angels, real angels are God's messengers, aren't they? The tatted angels all have God's word attached to them."

I milled this over in my mind. "There's been an explosion of angels lately. I mean, people write books about them. During Christmas last year the paper where I work did a two-day piece on angel stories. The angels they described, let's just say they weren't like any angels I ever read about, not in the Bible."

"I think," Sandy sighed, "that the world takes a different view of angels, different at least from Christians. I mean, they aren't meant for worship. If an angel appears, other than Christ, and the angel is worshiped, the person worshiping is quickly told not to do it."

"My momma always said angels don't have wings or halos either."

"When they appear in the Bible, they are recognizable, but at the same time they're like man," Sandy reasoned. "But, if Momma Roberts had received a tatted man with a verse, it wouldn't have been as special."

I smiled at the thought. "True."

"There's someone else who received an angel. You might want to avoid talking to him about it, but you probably want to visit him."

I waited.

"Seth," she lowered her head. "I think the last time Mickey wrote to you he told you Seth was getting married."

"Don't tell me he's getting a divorce, too. Those quick marriages never last."

"Michael, she died. She had the same type of cancer Momma's fighting. It was diagnosed, and it took her within two months. She didn't seek treatment in time. No one can figure out why. She and Seth would have been married a year Thanksgiving Day."

Seth's loss consumed my thoughts as I drove out of town to do the errands I planned. I thought of the young boy he had been. He was always gentle and kind and devoted to his father. Theirs was a bond much like the bond between my father and I, but I suspected their attachment was made stronger by the loss of Seth's mother well before he could remember her.

I wondered why he failed to notice Hannah's faithful love for him and had chosen the affections of another. I held no doubt that the love Seth shared with his wife was real and true, and it must have been tragic to lose her so suddenly after starting a new life together. Sandy never said so, but I felt that Seth had pulled away from those who cared for him. I wondered if he would accept my hand of friendship.

As kids, and even teenagers, we were friends, but our relationship was nothing compared to the friendship I forged with Mickey Roberts. Even though Mickey and I were estranged, I still knew that I could count on him with no questions asked. Seth's best friend was Jesse, and I wondered just how good a friend Jesse Crum could be with the life he was apparently leading. A sadness settled deep inside me over Seth's loss, and I knew that I would have to see him, to offer him friendship when it was probably the last thing he wanted. I remembered how he made time for me after my mother's death. He wasn't very good at comforting a friend, but he tried, and that was important. "She was a nice woman," he offered. "She made the best chocolate chip cookies I ever tasted." His words were meant to offer me peace, but they depressed me even more. Still, when he left, the comfort was in knowing I had a friend, and like Mickey and Jesse, he would always be there.

I finished my errands at the printing supply store on the mainland and headed home. My thoughts as I traveled in that direction turned to Valley. Sandy knew me too well. I had been more anxious to see Valley than I had been to renew my friendship with her brother. I could see Valley's battered face and recall her refusal to accept help. I tried to reason with myself that it was the situation in which she found herself. It was the syndrome of most every battered woman. I was angry with her all over again for her refusal of me. I was hurt that she still held the childhood fears of a teenager against me. I wished with all my heart that I could return to that day when I fled her schoolgirl advances. If I only had that one day, I would fall on my knees before her and vow to protect her from everything evil life had to offer, and Brad Rasneck would never have the opportunity to harm her.

If only, if only, if only, those words ran through my mind, and I was in a miserable state as I pulled into my yard. The cars were lining the road. I was startled at first; afraid my father needed help while I was away. I barely remember putting the old truck in park and running up the porch steps. "What's the hurry, Son?" A familiar voice stopped me.

Seth New's father, Jake, leaned against the porch post. He was my father's best friend, and I laughed often over tales of their fishing trips when they usually returned home without any catch at all. "The only ones that got a bite were the mosquitoes," my father roared over the phone while I sat in Detroit wishing for the opportunity to fish along with him.

I moved toward Jake and gave his hand a hearty shake, somewhat settled by his apparent relaxed state. "How are you?"

"Fine. We stopped by to congratulate your Dad on the paper. We really missed it. He told us you put it together. It's good to have you back."

"Jake, why didn't anyone tell me he was too ill to run the paper?"

"Respect for his wishes. What did bring you back here, Boy?" His tone was as southern as a man born this far south could be. He called every young man, "Son" or "Boy."

"I got news from a friend," I divulged little. "I heard about Seth's loss today. How is he doing?"

"He's in bad shape, Michael," his tone grew serious. "He won't step foot in their home. He lives on his boat. He's drinking heavily." The older man ran a hand across his beard. "And for a Christmas present, the town council is having a special vote to decide if they feel he's competent to perform his duties." He stared past me in silence for several moments. "It may be too late, but I know he'll come around. We all do once there's nothing left to lose." Deep inside, I felt that Jake spoke from experience.

"Has anyone been able to talk to him?"

Jake's gray eyes stared through me as if I were not there. "Hannah, her mother, me." He blinked as if to clear his mind then swallowed hard. "I remember when I lost my wife." He pushed away from the post where he had been leaning. "One man and his lady were gutsy enough to cut through my grief and put me back on track." He threw a thumb over his shoulder pointing toward the door. "Your father and your mother showed me a lot about myself. I had to face things. I had to realize that what was left after I screwed up was a healthy baby boy who needed me more than I needed the bottle." He shook his head as if clearing away the memories, and I wondered if he felt guilty for his wife's death. "Seth doesn't feel he's needed. He doesn't have a child like I did to help him see that he is important."

"I'll make a special point to see him, Jake."

"Don't be too surprised if his anger speaks louder than his true feelings."

"Well, he is needed. I've heard he's a darn good fireman, and he has friends here who'd miss him if he crawled into a bottle and didn't come out of it."

Jake placed a hand on my shoulder as the screen door opened and several of my father's other friends emerged. They congratulated my work and left quickly. I found my father alert but tired as he sat in his chair in the living room. He smiled as I entered, "Errands took awhile?"

"No," I told him. "I stopped by to visit Mrs. Roberts."

"She's a fighter that Sabrina."

With his words, my miserable mood returned just as quickly as I thought it left me. "I'm getting a glass of water. Would you like something?" He shook his head, and I moved to the kitchen, poured the

water and sat staring out the window for a long while. I could see the
offices of the *Serenade* down the road. It needed painting. There was
a lot more to be done than digging up the news and running the paper
once a week. Things had been left to run down.

It occurred to me that my father's friends all knew the truth I
refused to accept. Unlike Sabrina Roberts, Trevor Abernathy was not
fighting. He was putting up a facade to make people believe otherwise, but every day, I watched him slip away from me in just the same
way that Mickey and Sandy watched Sabrina. There was only one difference, Sabrina was not ready to go and Trevor was. I drank the glass
of water down quickly. I had every intention of confronting him. I
would retrieve the old paper given to me by Ted at the *Ledger*. I would
demand to know why he was giving up now when he hadn't given up
back then after he lost his brother's family, when he had not even
given up when my mother died.

My intentions were forgotten as I returned to the living room. My
gaze fell upon an object sitting on the table beside my father's chair. I
stopped abruptly then stumbled forward. My hand reached out. My
fingers grasped it. "Many waters cannot quench love. Neither can
floods drown it. If a man would give all the substance of his house for
love, it would utterly be contemned." Song of Solomon 8:7.

The angel I held was of the brightest, boldest red I could recall ever
seeing. The work was exquisite, another masterpiece of double knots
and picots. Its face was an unpainted wooden ball that added to its
charm in the same way it had Sabrina's angel. "Dad?" I moved in front
of him holding the angel. "Where did you get this?"

My father eyed the angel as if never setting eyes on it before. "I don't
know. Where did it come from?"

"Here, on your table. Do you know that someone has been leaving
these for other people?"

"I've heard."

"With a Bible verse. Does this verse mean anything to you?" I
handed the angel to him.

"Is it supposed to?" He read it quickly.

"I thought so. I thought that was the idea." I told him of Sabrina's
verse and what Sandy had said about Blanchie's verse. I purposely did

not mention the fact that Seth may also have received an angel. I was sure Jake had not burdened my father with Seth's sorrows.

He thought long and hard for a while then shook his head. "Maybe this angel isn't for me."

"It has to be. One of your friends left it here just now."

My father's laughter was mocking but very sweet to my ears. "You honestly think that one of those men..." He coughed. "That's a riot." He handed the angel back to me, and I had to laugh. There was not one of my father's friends who would be caught dead delivering something so unmanly.

"I guess I have my work cut out for me."

"What's that?" His question was sharp.

"I promised Mrs. Roberts I'd find out who our angel of mercy happens to be."

"Some things are better left to mystery. The legend is sometimes the better story, and the truth better left to imagination."

"You're saying there isn't a story in this?"

"No, what I'm saying is that you may have a slant that's more interesting."

I looked at the angel. Its color was enticing but yet not at all the color for an angel. "You mean the story of why, not who?"

"There it is!" His eyes twinkled.

"What?" I looked around to see what he discovered.

"The money your mother and I spent on your college education. I see it at work!"

I made a face as if the joke held no humor, but as I walked out the door on my way to the *Serenade* I know he could hear my laughter. Trevor Abernathy's sense of humor was still intact, and it helped alleviate the foul mood I harbored only moments before.

My step was light. I had a purpose, a story. There was real work to be done. I was what some might call a very happy camper. I would find the where, what and who of this mystery, and I would print it in the *Serenade*. Thus, my search for the story behind the appearance of the Serenity Key tatted angels began.

Chapter Four

Angels In Green

"To everything there is a season, and a time to every purpose under heaven… A time to cast away stones, and a time to gather stones together; a time to embrace, and a time to refrain from embracing; A time to get, and a time to lose; a time to keep, and a time to cast away." - Ecclesiastes 3: 1 & 5-6.

My plan was to write the article for the Christmas Eve edition. I studied my notes from my conversations with Sabrina and Sandy. My next step would be to interview Blanchie Crum.

Georgie suddenly appeared two days into my work on the following week's edition. He was genuinely glad to see me and spent a long while battering me with questions about my life in Detroit. Once he exhausted all possible inquiries, I put the man to work helping with both my father and with the paper. My generous offer of pay did not seem to faze Georgie. His true pleasure in life was to help others.

My work in Detroit taught me to write within deadlines, to cover all angles, but I had been spoiled by the fact that all I was required to do was write the story. Others worried with the printing and the advertisements. In fact, many people worried about each aspect of the *Ledger*. I could not begin to tell you who worked for that organization or, in fact, who owned the paper.

I was quickly reminded that in order for the *Serenade* to make money, we needed advertisers. I actually ran the first copy using older advertising. It had been free for the local businesses, and for that reason, there was not one complaint. Even the ads offering discounts were readily acceptable by the merchants. I contacted those same sponsors and procured their promise of advertising dollars. Once their business was secured, I changed their advertising to fit their specifications, many reflecting Holiday specials. This all proved to be a bigger burden than I remembered. I was very thankful that Georgie was around to take over most of the manual labor. He was very good at following directions and work on the paper progressed until my second full issue was printed and most of the Holiday changes behind me.

Blanchie was not difficult to find. All I had to do was make the much-needed appointment to have my hair trimmed. She must have sensed my reason for coming because I found her tatted angel sitting on her workstation in her salon. "My father received an angel," I remarked as I sat.

Blanchie picked up her angel and handed it to me. It was a brilliant Christmas green. I read the verses even though I knew what they said. "Sandy said you might stop in." She stopped the charade that I barely noticed I was playing. In Detroit it was the way stories were written. In Serenity the best approach was honesty, and Blanchie slyly reminded me of just that. I watched as she combed my hair into place readying for the cut. "Blanchie, what do angels mean to you?"

There wasn't a second of hesitation before she announced her understanding. "God uses them to deliver us from situations." My face must have told her that I did not understand. Always with Blanchie, her reasoning was so simplistic it was hard to grasp. "For he shall give his angels charge over thee, to keep thee in all thy ways," she repeated a Bible verse probably learned in Sabrina's class. "They watch over us."

"Yeah, go on," I knew where she was going, but I wanted to hear it in her own words.

"Okay, you're driving down the road, and your mind is miles away. You're not paying attention and somewhere in the back of your mind you realize you had better pay attention. You become more alert and right at that moment you see a car barreling toward you that has no intention of stopping at the intersection. You slam on your brakes, and your life is saved. It was done because an angel whispered in your ear and saved your life."

Simple but profound, that was how I suddenly saw Blanchie. "What did this angel's verse say to you?" I pressed.

She started to cut my hair, and a smile of such peace appeared upon her face. "It was a reminder that sometimes God has to do the work. I could stay married to Jesse and watch him slowly kill himself and the love I have for him, or I could take away his comfort zone, me, and let him suffer so God can work in his life." She continued clipping my hair with expert attention to the details. Finishing the cut, she leaned over me to pull out the electric clippers. The words she spoke were profound for a girl who always seemed so childlike, everything in her life a wonder, a new discovery.

"Very mature thinking," I told her.

"One of us has to grow up," she spoke and her voice held a touch of bitterness. "But it was Jesse's dad who gave me the advice and the courage to leave the marriage." The clippers buzzed, and I leaned forward as she shaved the hairs on my neck. When she finished I raised my head. She smiled once again, and her face beamed back at me from the mirror. "I love him, you know." I did know she loved Jesse Crum, and even though Jesse might protest otherwise and complain that his wife was too controlling, there was not a doubt in my mind that my rascal of a friend adored his wife.

"Someday, if the Lord is willing, he'll come back," she removed the cover she used to protect my clothes from falling hair and brushed my shoulders. "But right now, he isn't open to anything the Lord could offer, and he will have to try very hard to win me back. I won't let him win too easily. I've always made things too easy for Jesse."

"How is he? How are you both doing?"

"He was angry at first, then he was apologetic. He's just resigned to the fact that the divorce will be finalized in a few days."

"How about you?"

"I think I've experienced the same stages Jesse went through. I received the angel in the second stage. I was ready to go back to Jesse and tell him I was sorry, and the message of the angel made me realize I was doing the right thing by standing my ground. Like I said, it reminded me that staying with him is not doing either one of us any good," she took the angel from my hand. "I could have the comfort of having him near me, but he wouldn't have the comfort of respecting me."

I stood and pulled out my wallet to pay for my cut. She would never cease to amaze me with her clarity. "I enjoyed talking with you. Thank you."

"I'm glad you're back," she walked with me to her cash register and placed the money inside. Closing the cash drawer she stepped around and kissed my cheek. "Jesse's at the cabin writing. If you get a chance, stop by to say hello to him."

"He's still writing?" I asked her out of politeness. I knew he would always be a writer. It was not a profession that you chose. Writers have a need to put words on paper. Their imaginations flood their brains and have to be stored on paper. I knew that personally because even in my dreams my mind worked on my story line. For the last few days, the tatted angels had captivated my thought process.

"He sold a book last year," her voice held the pride of a wife happy with her husband's accomplishments. "It didn't do too well, but he signed a contract for another one he submitted in proposal form."

"I'm sure I'll see him," I told her.

"You may want to see Turk Williams, too?"

Turk Williams, the name ran through my head. Was it possible that in my three years away, I had forgotten someone on the island? "I don't recall..."

"Oh, you wouldn't." Blanchie waved as her next customer entered. "Turk is Curt Davis' officer."

"And why would I want to visit him?"

"He has an angel."

It was too simple. I should have known. "Thank you," I smiled. "I'll see Turk."

I turned as Blanchie moved around to greet her customer. "Valley, it's been so long."

My eyes beheld her, but I could not believe that she was in front of me. Her face was healed with only a slight redness where her lip had been cut. As the weather had been projected to turn cooler, she was dressed in warmer clothing. I wondered if Corrine had purchased it for her out of the money I provided. If not, I was sure it was borrowed from her sister-in-law. "Hi," I managed to utter only one word. Her abrupt turn from me toward Blanchie was like a slap in my face. I opened the door and stepped into the December day that began considerably warmer and, as projected, had cooled to remind us that sometimes Old Man Winter did visit this far south.

The loud honk of the truck horn made me jump. I was irritated at first until the truck pulled to the curb and the man jumped out and ran to where I stood. I laughed at Jesse Crum as he stood in front of me wearing shorts and a thin shirt. "Man, it's cold," he stuffed his hands into his pockets. "I just saw Jake. He told me you were back. How are you?"

"I'm fine. I just learned you sold a book."

"Yeah, what was the title? I think the underlying theme was something about war and peace. I got $4.00 for it," his green eyes twinkled with humor. He was never serious.

"Okay, I misunderstood," I played along. "What are you doing so well dressed for the weather?"

"I called in an order to Jake's Place and just picked it up. The temperature dropped twenty degrees since I left home." He twisted and turned as the wind picked up. "It was good to see the paper up and running again. I'll have to call and put an ad in once I move back on the boat when it warms up. I think I'm leaving the garage behind. I want to do some general labor," he elbowed me. "You can't monopolize Georgie's talent. I think he and I can go into business together."

"Georgie's my partner," I uttered the retort. Georgie had become invaluable to me and to the paper. There was no way on God's green earth that I would let Jesse take him away from my father's business or my family.

"Georgie," Jesse said the name with fondness. "What would we all do without Georgie?"

"Considerably less than we do now."

"He's Seth's biggest volunteer."

"Speaking of Seth…"

"Don't," Jesse's lips changed quickly from a smile to a frown. "He's living in Hell, and I don't know how to pull him out, Michael." Never in all my years of knowing Jesse had I known him to show concern, but in front of me was a man determined to do anything to help our friend, if he could only find out what it was Seth needed from him.

"Have you tried talking with him?" Silly questions always come forth when you least expect them.

"Have I tried?" Jesse took exception to my stupidity. "Of course, I've tried. Man, he's making me take a look at myself. At least I'm a happy drinker. He just sits in his sorrows when he drinks."

"Would it do any good if I went to see him?"

"I just saw him, Michael, and he's in no mood for company. I doubt he'd remember you even stopped by," he jumped up and down against the cold. "Did you drive in?"

"No, I walked." Jesse's cabin was pretty far out in the brush, and I did not blame him for driving in to town, but most natives walked.

"Get in. I'll give you a ride," he hurried back to the truck before I could decline.

I opened the door. "I have a stop to make. I can walk."

"I'll drop you off," he urged as he turned the heater on full blast. "Where to, Friend?"

"I'm heading to Mickey's house."

"Ah, family," he joked. "My favorite sister and brother-in-law," he pulled away from the curb barely giving me time to get inside. "They've been real good to me through this."

"They care about you," I told him nothing he did not already know.

"That's what I mean. I don't deserve their kindness. Mickey told me time and time again that Blanchie was going to leave me if I didn't change."

"Why don't you change?"

He didn't answer. I looked out the window. Christmas was beginning to come to the island. Families were outside bundled against the sudden cold. They strung lights in trees and on houses. Christmas trees were beginning to show up in the windows of homes, but as we pulled up in front of the Roberts' home, I realized that at this home, there would be no season of joy. "It would be too easy," Jesse broke through my thoughts.

"I'm sorry." I did not realize he was contemplating our conversation. This introspection from my easy-going friend took me by surprise.

"Changing would be too easy," he sat with his hand on the steering wheel, "kind of like salvation."

He was suddenly too deep in his thoughts. I wanted to look around to see if somehow we hadn't slipped into a parallel world where everyone you knew was the exact opposite of who they actually were. This new Jesse was confusing.

"Salvation is too easy, isn't it?"

This was one conversation I never expected to have with Jesse, Mickey, yes, Jesse, never. "The ones who accept it seem to think that way. I mean it is God's gift. He opens our eyes to it, and he gives it to us." I found myself sounding almost like a preacher. Knowing Jesse's father was a pastor, I was sure that the last thing the man wanted was a sermon. He never seemed to listen before. Still, I pressed on, "But for those people who don't have their eyes opened and their hearts remain closed, it's the most difficult thing to understand."

"I'm saved," his voice was low as if the words he spoke deserved reverence, "But it just seems too easy to believe that God forgives everything I've done."

"You're the worst sinner I have ever known," I smiled at him mischievously, not meaning a word I said. We had been taught much differently. "Besides me," I corrected. "You just need to talk with God."

"Have you talked with him lately?" There was no hint of sarcasm in his voice.

"No, Jess, I haven't."

"When you do, will you tell him that I really need to talk to him and would he drop in sometime? Remind him about Seth, too."

The tale-tale sign of moistness in his eyes told me he was not teasing. The preacher's son was pleading with me for intervention. "Sure," I nodded as I started to open the door.

"Hey," he stopped me and leaned over. He pulled open the glove compartment and reached inside. "Sandy mentioned you were looking for people who have these," he tossed a tatted angel in my lap. It was the same green as his wife's angel, and it held the same verses. "To everything there is a season and a time to every purpose under the heaven. A time to cast away stones and a time to gather stones together, a time to embrace and a time to refrain from embracing. A time to get and a time to lose, a time to keep and a time to cast away, Ecclesiastes 3:1, 5 & 6," I read it aloud. "Did you know that Blanchie received the same verses with an identical angel?"

His only answer was a nod.

"What does it mean to you?"

"It reminded me that I was casting away something that means life or death to me. She does, you know. I found out too late that Blanchie Higgs is my world."

"Then why are you letting her go?"

"Because I love her," he took the angel back from me, "And I've done so much to her that she doesn't even know. I owe her freedom from me."

The depth of the love that this couple held for each other was amazing to me. They loved each other so much that Blanchie was cutting the strings to save her husband, and Jesse was letting them fall in order to save his wife from any further hurt. I thought about talking with God and about asking him to piece them back together better than new. Blanchie's wisdom resounded in my mind. God had to do it or it wouldn't work out. "Jesse, don't stay a stranger. Let's go fishing soon."

"After the holidays," he promised, "when it's warmer."

I nodded as I got out of the truck then I looked back inside. "What do you think God's purpose is for angels?"

He shook his head and gave me a blank stare. "I don't have any idea."

Honesty would someday be his best quality, but my unsatisfied curiosity was not happy with his answer. I closed the door and waved. For the first time in our lives, I knew I had seen a side of Jesse he seldom showed. He was hurting. He was calling out for help, and I wanted to help him. The only trouble was, I didn't know where to start.

Chapter Five

Angel In Yellow

"For thou hast delivered my soul from death: wilt not
thou deliver my feet from falling, that I may walk before
God in the land of the living?" Psalm 56:13

I intended on visiting Officer Turk Williams immediately, but plans
and actions often travel different paths. With Valley away from the
house, I thought it would be the best time to call on Mrs. Roberts. She
was sitting up, alert and happy now that Valley had returned home.
Her breathing was better, and her demeanor hid the fact that she was
a dying woman. "Mickey told me you found her," she reached out her
hand, and I held to it.

"It was a coincidence," I advised.

"God works in mysterious ways. Most often we think it coincidence. Still, Michael, thank you. I was praying I'd see her again. God
used you to answer my prayers."

One nod from Mickey told me that Sabrina Roberts knew nothing
of the squalor in which her daughter chose to live. "I'm glad she's
home. I just saw her in town. She's looking very good."

"Have you been able to find out about my angel?" Sabrina changed
the subject.

I shook my head, "But I'm working on it."

Sabrina looked to her son who sat on the windowsill, moody and
contemplating. "Mickey, if I'm not around when Michael finds this
person, I want you to tell him or her how much it meant to me."

"Momma, you have a long time yet," Mickey's words were far from convincing. He was tired. Normally, Mickey stood or sat tall and proud. Now, his shoulders were stooped, and his eyes held a deep sadness. I sympathized with him. I had been the most fortunate. If my mother had to be taken, I was spared watching her die daily, torn between wanting her to have the peace that came with death, and wanting her to be near. It struck me suddenly that Mickey's father had been taken quickly, whereas my father was very slowly slipping away, and like Mickey, I did not want to see him go.

"I'm glad to see you looking so well today," I focused my attention on Sabrina. "And I'll stop in again. Next time, I'll have more to tell you about the angels."

"I look forward to it," she released the grasp she had on my hand.

I gave a wave toward Mickey as I left his mother's room. There was still tension between us, and I felt that he did not feel the need to repair the damage that kept us apart.

Sandy was in the kitchen preparing dinner. Her motions, the excessive banging of pots, the quick slam of cabinets told me she was angry. I was not prepared for the tears I saw when she turned. "What is it?" I asked.

"If she doesn't want to be here, why did she come back?" She spat. "She shows one face to her mother, all nice and sweet, and then she hurts Mickey with accusations and lies. You're so lucky she walked out of your life."

I didn't see it that way, but I remained silent. Sandy's emotions were boiling over, and they needed to be spent.

"She's angry with you, you know. She's just sure you're the reason Brad is still in jail. It was you and Mickey. It was some great conspiracy having absolutely nothing to do with his prior record or her injuries!" She stood, her hands over her face.

"He's still in jail?" The words fell out of my mouth with utter surprise. Corrine must have done as I asked.

"He refused to plea guilty when he saw Mickey in court. He was sure Valley called him to post bail," her laugh was as bitter as her words. "He was surprised when Mickey refused, and he even threatened Valley in front of Mick, but does that wake her up? Oh, no.

Mickey had to practically carry her back here to see her own mother before she dies."

"It's not all her fault," I began.

The fury that sprang into Sandy's eyes caused me to step back. "Oh, don't you pull that forgiving attitude on me," she pointed angrily. "I don't care if she thinks that his treatment of her is his way of expressing love. What I do care about is that she hurt you, and she tore you and Mickey apart. I care that there is a woman upstairs that gave Valley life and cared for her and loved her, and she's so self-centered that she believes she's being punished because she has to visit and offer some comfort. Momma could be taken away any minute, and Valley and I are all Mickey will have," tears streamed down her face. "I'll never forgive her! Never!"

I wrapped the anguished woman in my arms. She sobbed against me until she could cry no longer. Then she pushed away. "I'm sorry," she wiped her eyes with the back of her hand. "I love so much that when I hate it tears me apart."

"You don't hate her. You're angry." I offered my best smile, tipping her chin up with my index finger. "I have someone to see about an angel. Why don't you tell Mickey you're going with me?"

She thought for a long moment.

"When's the last time you stepped out of the house?" I encouraged.

"Go on," Mickey stood at the bottom of the back stairs. He moved to his wife, and I wondered how long he had been there. "I'll finish dinner."

"Let me wash up," Sandy went up the stairs, and it was obvious that all she needed was his approval, not because Mickey was demanding, but because she didn't want to leave her husband alone if he needed her near.

"Thanks," Mickey went to the refrigerator. Because I was unsure of the reason for his gratitude, I simply nodded. "Momma said you read the paper to her. I never realized it was so important."

"I couldn't think of anything else to do."

Mickey took a pitcher of tea from the refrigerator, poured a glass. He held the pitcher toward me offering me a glass. When I refused, he sat the pitcher down and leaned his tall frame against the counter. I hated the uncomfortable feeling that settled between us. "Sandy's under a lot of stress," he commented, and I wanted to tell him that I knew he was, too.

"I see that."

"I haven't been able to work. Studying for the Bar Exam is a joke. I have a law degree, but it's useless to me right now. I had such great plans for this Christmas, and money's very tight. What little we had, I used to get Valley back home."

"Well, Mickey, it doesn't pay much, but there's room in the *Serenade* for an article, say some legal information, or just about anything you can offer." I was making it up as I went along, and it began to sound good. "A column, maybe something..."

"I know," he smiled for the first time. "Anything I can make up so that you can pay me, and it won't look like charity."

"Exactly. Deadline tomorrow at 5:00 p.m."

We both laughed and when I held my hand out in friendship Mickey pulled me into a brotherly embrace that melted the uneasiness. At that moment, I remembered an unspoken contract we entered into many years ago. The terms needed no pronouncement. We were friends, and friends would always be around when things were at their best and when they were at their worse. Our paths took different directions for a while, and we were growing, but I silently vowed we would never grow apart again.

Sandy returned a few moments later and kissed her husband good-bye. "Watch this guy," he warned her. "He likes to entertain damsels in distress." If Sandy had not been present, a few choice words might have been thrown in her husband's direction and my vow would have been broken.

It was obvious that Sandy and Sally Williams were friends, but I felt strange from the moment the officer's wife opened her front door and bid us welcome. Sally was happy to have a visit from Sandy but very leery of the fact that her friend brought a stranger with her. Children, their faces gleaming, were helping their mother with Christmas decorations. Ornaments, ribbons and lights were unpacked and laid about the living room floor. There was a spot cleared in the corner of the room, but the tree was missing. "It will be our first real Christmas tree. Turk said he wanted to celebrate this Christmas in style because we have so much to be thankful for this year," Mrs. Williams explained.

"Sally, I'd like you to meet Michael Abernathy. Michael and his father own the local paper, the *Serenade*."

"Oh." Confusion was evident on the woman's face. "You must be Mr. Abernathy's son. He's such a nice man."

I wondered how Mrs. Williams knew my father, but I remained silent.

"Michael wanted to talk to Turk about the angel."

Brightness filled the woman's charcoal colored eyes. "The angel," she bid us sit and commanded the children to either play quietly inside or put their coats on and play outside. As they scampered off, she apologized needlessly for the disorder in her home. "We don't have many guests. Curt is underfoot a lot, but I think of him as family."

"Curt only has his aunt, so I bet your family is special to him," Sandy remarked.

"And he is special to us," she assured. "But he has good friends in Lonnie Culver and Bella Edwards, too." I immediately wondered if the name of Bella's fiancé was omitted on purpose. Noah McGowan and Curt Davis were inseparable when we were teenagers. I don't know when we stopped thinking of Curt as a newcomer to the island. He was seven or eight when he moved with his aunt to Serenity, but in order to obtain true citizen status, the town folk must have forgotten when you actually arrived. From the start, Noah introduced Curt to everyone and made him feel welcome. Now, I sensed something was wrong. My journalistic mind wondered if there was a story behind the reason Bella and Noah were not married and if Curt might be the reason for a possible broken engagement.

Sally Williams settled into a chair across from the couch where Sandy and I sat. "Curt took a chance, a big chance hiring my big man." Her words brought me back to the matter at hand.

"Did your husband interview for the job?" I asked out of curiosity remembering Mickey's correspondence.

"No. Curt and my husband were at the academy at the same time. Turk never realized Curt even knew him, but after Curt was elected

Chief of Police here, he called and offered him the job. He told us he needed a man that people would fear immediately."

"Some comment," I laughed, but as the door opened, and the man entered with the six-foot Frazier Fir, I knew exactly what Curt Davis meant. Turk Williams stood no less than six feet, eight inches tall, and his build was like a wall of stone. His voice, even in jolly respite, was deep and commanding. I stood as he maneuvered the tree single handedly.

"Michael," Curt Davis stood behind his officer, but I had been unable to see him. Turk's large frame hid him completely. "How are you?"

I stood and shook his hand. "I'm fine. It's good to see you."

"I enjoyed the paper last week. It's good to have you back."

Turk Williams placed the tree firmly in the stand and held it while Sally secured the bottom. That done as easily as if he did this sort of thing every day he turned to his guests and shook my hand. A sheepish grin crossed his face as he realized that the pinesap transferred from the tree to his skin stuck easily to mine. He hesitated, but Sandy gave him a hug, her tiny arms too small to reach around him. "Good to see you, Mrs. Roberts," he said with manners that marked him a true southerner. "How is your mother-in-law?"

"Not good, but I see you're recovering well."

"Even if I wasn't, I wouldn't let those two good old boys know." The large man stopped his wife as she returned with the water for their new tree. She stood on the tips of her toes and kissed his lips tenderly. "My angel goes on the tree first," he demanded lovingly.

"That's why Mr. Abernathy came by," Sally announced.

Turk left the room suddenly without a word. Sally bent to water the tree, and I looked to Sandy who shrugged. Curt Davis offered a smile for both of us. Turk returned as Sally stood from watering the tree. He handed the bright yellow angel to me. As always, I read the verse, "For thou hast delivered my soul from death; wilt not thou deliver my feet from falling, that I may walk before God in the light of the living, Psalm 56:13." I held it up, examined it. Except for the color it was the identical pattern of all the other angels. The work was definitely that of one person.

"God bless that soul." Sally Williams sighed. "God bless them."

"You came close to death?" I inquired.

Curt Davis straightened. "I thought I lost a good, good friend."

Turk bent his large frame and picked up a strand of lights. He held them out and examined them. It was obvious he did not feel comfortable with our conversation. "Mr. Abernathy, I'm a likeable man. I have a strong belief in God. I fought in the Gulf War. I love my country. I have learned to love this town, but when a man, any man, threatens my wife and my children I will risk my life to defend them as strongly as I defended God and country."

"I wasn't here," I informed him. "I haven't heard."

Turk laid the strand of lights down. He reached out and took the angel. "I knew I wouldn't be accepted. I told Curt that when he offered me the job, and he was honest. He said it would be tough, but he wanted me. So, I came because he showed a faith in me few men have ever shown.

Sally and I came here, and we decided it would be a good place for our kids to grow," he studied his gift. "Curt was wrong. We may not have been welcomed with open arms, but we experienced very little open hostility. We have one good friend, and I'd rather have that friendship than a hundred others." He looked to where Curt started to unwind the strand of lights Turk had discarded. "But there's always some who openly hate..."

"Todd Rasneck and his brother, Carl, caught Turk on patrol around by the *Serenade* about six weeks ago. They'd been very vocal about not having Turk on Serenity, and there were threats made against Sally and the kids. When they saw Turk patrolling alone, I think they thought they'd rough him up, but Turk was too much for them to handle. When they saw that the odds were not in their favor, Carl pulled a gun." Curt explained, and it did not surprise me that Brad's older brothers were so criminally inclined.

I was shocked both by what I heard and by my first reaction. This man had been shot on my father's property. Still, two words ran through my mind. *Real news.* I missed real news. It was Turk's movement as he pulled up his shirt that reminded me of the tragedy of the story. How he had carried the tree with the wound that was still evident on his side eluded me. Yet, I realized immediately that one inch was the difference between life and death," Turk lowered his shirt. "The angel was left in my hospital room."

"Can you remember who visited?"

"That's the great thing." Turk smiled to where his wife was re-entering the room.

Unnoticed, both women had left. Sally now returned with a plate of sandwiches. Sandy followed with a tray carrying cups of hot liquid for everyone. "All the town folks showed their support of Turk by visiting him or calling or sending cards and flowers. Your father was so sweet. He felt responsible for what happened, and he made Jake New drive him to the hospital to apologize to Turk personally," Sally beamed, and I smiled easily. That was just like my father, and so like the town I knew and loved. I would have expected nothing less. "He received so many cards and letters, we had to box them," Sally continued.

"But this angel, and her verse, they just mean so much. They told me not to give up."

"God bless that person," Sally repeated. She handed me a cup of hot chocolate, and I welcomed it. From outside, as if on cue, the three children ran inside. Without a thought, Sandy and I were drawn into a celebration of family and friendship stringing lights, wrapping the garland and helping to place each decoration on the tree. We enjoyed the Williams' explanation for their family ornaments and what each meant to them. It was so enjoyable that neither Sandy nor I noticed that darkness had descended until the tree was lit and the room illuminated against the black night outside the window.

As we prepared to leave, I asked one last question of Turk, and it took a lot of soul searching before he answered. "Protectors," he told me. "Angels are God's defenders. Obviously, they saved me, but they fight for us in realms unseen," his eyes shined. "The Archangel Michael is my kind of angel!" He pulled his tiny wife to him and extended his arm toward me. "I enjoyed tonight."

My hand was engulfed in his large dark one. It seemed strange that when I first entered his home, the skin color of this family caused me to be uncomfortable, but leaving their company, I knew I just made very good friends. I understood that my feelings were a reflection upon me, and I was ashamed. "Good night, Turk," I walked out into the night. It had turned even colder, and Sandy and I walked briskly.

"Hey," Curt ran behind us. We stopped. He wore no jacket, and I wondered if a little of Jesse Crum had not rubbed off on Curt through the years. "Are you looking for other angels?" He asked.

I nodded, "Yeah, I am."

"You might want to see Noah. Bella told me he received one. There's a great story there."

"What's going on with them?" I couldn't help but ask.

Curt's green eyes darted from Sandy and back to me. He wasn't sure how much we knew, and I assumed he didn't want to divulge too much. "The question should be what's going on between them."

"Okay, Curt, what's going on between Noah and Annabella?"

"Me," he said, and Sandy gasped. His cheeks blazed red. "It's not like that, Sandy."

"What is it like?" She spat. "When Rosa told Momma she thought you and Bella were carrying on, I told her that it was impossible. Bella loves Noah."

"Bella does love Noah," his voice held strong conviction.

"Then why are you still hanging around her? You're making things difficult for them." In her protective mode, Sandy was like a bear with her cub.

"If Noah would try to understand, if he would look back at all the years we've been friends, he'd know the truth."

"Which is...." Sandy leaned forward as if she expected a much better explanation.

"I can't—- I can't tell you any more than I can tell him, but Bella has never betrayed Noah. She loves him. This is killing her. I think the angel helped, though." It was obvious that he wanted to make us understand, but he could tell us nothing more. "You may want to talk to him, Michael, and if he asks, you tell him what I said about Bella," he turned and left us, his head bowed.

Sandy and I walked along slowly, both reflecting silently on what Curt divulged. It wasn't until we were almost to her home that she spoke. "Blanchie said you asked her the same question you asked Turk and me. Why is it so important to know what the angels mean to us?"

"There's not much in the Bible about them." I knew that because I conducted some research. "And it seems that everyone has an idea of what the angels do, and a lot of what they think isn't biblical at all."

"What have you gotten from others so far?"

"Protector, guardian, your messenger, and Jesse said he had no idea."

"Jesse, did he receive one?"

I assumed Jesse had told her, but obviously he failed to do so. "He received a green angel with the same verse your sister received

"That's all interesting, isn't it?" We came to her walkway. "I had fun tonight." She looked toward the house that was mostly dark. "We don't even have a tree this year."

"You should."

"No time," her shoulders seemed to sag.

I nodded and thought about my own home. Dad did not want a tree, and the thought of it seemed to tire him. He had been so happy about the approaching Holiday when I first arrived, but his enthusiasm waned as it neared. I gave in easily simply because I was too busy myself.

"Do you want to come in?" Sandy's voice broke into my thoughts.

"No, I need to go home and make sure Dad's eaten," I started away but turned to see her still staring sadly toward the house. "Sandy, did Mickey's mom ever say what the angel means to her?"

"No, she didn't," she lowered her head then looked back to me. She wiped briskly at a falling tear. "But seeing that verse and that angel everyday has given her more comfort than you can imagine, Michael." She straightened, and with all the strength she could muster, she stepped toward the sadness that had become her home.

Chapter Six

Angel Of Rose

"Thou therefore, my son, be strong in the grace
that is in Christ Jesus." - II Timothy 2:1

*D*ad was asleep in the recliner when I returned home. He stirred, and I coaxed him to bed. While he slept, I wrote. I found my mother's books on tatting procedure and patterns. Using them as a reliable reference I was able to explain the intricate art of tatting. As a boy, I watched my mother tat, and the fluid movement of her hands and fingers fascinated me. She explained that it was a series of double knots made by moving the shuttle under and then over a thread held by the opposite hand. She taught the art for awhile, and many women gave up rather than stick with it, but those who finally got the idea seemed to form a close knit group who shared the patterns they found as well as created. I discovered a list of names, and realized that all of the women my mother taught were no longer in Serenity.

Pattern upon pattern lay in my mother's boxes. Some I recognized as items she made and sold at the craft store on the dock area of town. Their instructions might as well have been Greek to me, and I struggled to understand. Finally, in frustration I satisfied myself by moving on to the heart of my article, the angels and the people they affected. It was 4:00 a.m. when I wrote the last word, stood, stretched, and went off to bed for a few hours rest.

When I woke at 10:00 a.m., I found my father already awake. He sat at the table, his eyes skimming over the papers I left there. "This is well written," he praised. "There is one slant you missed, though."

"What?" I poured a cup of coffee from the pot he had prepared. I yawned, scratched my head and moved to peer over his shoulder.

"So far, each of your angels is a different color, except for the two given to Blanchie and Jesse."

"Yeah?" I waited for him to continue.

"Could there be a reason?"

I thought on it for a long moment. "Could be."

"Maybe you should look into that," he became the Senior Editor and for some reason, I liked it.

"It might be an interesting angle," I nodded.

"Why didn't you write about the red angel?"

I struggled with just that subject the night before. "Because it just doesn't make sense. I still have a while before the Christmas Eve issue, and I'll put some thought into it."

"Awe!" He said loudly. "Another adventure."

I laughed. "Yeah, I assume so."

I waited until after lunch to assure my father received a good meal before I walked over to the *Serenade*. The typical weather pattern for the area was cold one day, hot the next, and it held true. I wore a jacket but it was quickly discarded when I reached the office. Georgie was there sweeping up the floor. "You're late," he scolded.

"I'm sorry, Boss," I held up my article. "But I worked late last night."

"Jesse Crum needs me today." The overgrown man-child stated his question in the form of a statement. "That okay?" He swept the broom across the floor in exaggerated movements.

"Sure, Georgie." He was aggravated, and I didn't understand. "Is something bothering you?"

"Mr. Seth, he's in big trouble."

"Seth New?"

Georgie nodded, swept more vigorously.

"What kind of trouble?"

"I heard Mr. Jake. He said the town council don't want him no more. Mr. Seth, he's not a bad man. He's just hurt. Ms. Linda, she was beautiful. He's crying for her. He misses his Ms. Linda."

Everyone in Georgie's life was Mister or Miss. His mother had drummed that into him and nothing would change it. If a person appeared to be of an age of respect, Georgie gave them a title. "Will you talk to Mr. Seth, Mr. Mike?"

There it was, the dreaded nickname. For me, personally, I never liked the shortened version of my name, but Georgie was stubborn, and it remained my title. "I'll see if I can get by." Guilt coursed through me like a shockwave when you touch unguarded electricity. I meant to visit Seth, and I failed to do so.

"Mr. Seth, he's a nice man. He's just like you. He's sad because he's lost someone he loves, just like you're sad because Ms. Valley doesn't love you." He put the broom down oblivious to the arrow he just shot through my heart. I wondered if my pain was so obvious to everyone. "I'm going to see Mr. Trevor first. He said he had an errand for me."

"You have a good day." I watched him run clumsily down the road toward my home. Refusing to dwell on his observation, I set to work. It was hard work, but toward 4:00 p.m. I had the paper ready with the exception of Mickey's article. Thinking he had forgotten, I picked up the phone. As I did, the door opened, and Mickey entered. He held the two typewritten pages in his hand, apologizing before I read them, explaining his motives. "It's not very long, but it does say what needs to be said." I almost had to yank the pages from him. "It's not exactly what you wanted."

I read his work, devouring the words with passion, sympathy, and a deep understanding of his meaning. When I finished, I looked up to him. He was staring out the dirty window of the office. "Are you sure you want me to print this?" It was well written, but I didn't need to tell him that. He knew. It came from his heart.

"No," he did not turn toward me, and I saw that he was staring at my reflection in the glass. "It's just a truth I need to express to some-one I love very much." I understood. I set to work and before long had the paper ready to run the next day.

Mickey stayed and watched for a while, but he became weary about leaving his mother for so long. He left and after I finished up, I walked home. My father sat in his chair with a plate of food before him watching television. He advised that Georgie had delivered two such plates from Jake New's restaurant. Mine was in the oven on warm. I retrieved my meal and sat in the living room with him. "I found something today," he looked up from his plate. "When were you going to tell me that you know about your Uncle Carl?"

I choked down the last spoonful of food I had placed into my mouth without chewing. "You went into my coat pocket?" I decided that I would challenge him to throw him off guard. It never worked when I was younger. It sure didn't work this time.

"Georgie was helping me clean up. He picked up your coat and heard the paper rustle inside. He pulled it out and brought it to me," he shook his head. It was his silent way of telling me that my ploy failed. "That explained, Mister, you have some explaining of your own to do."

"No," I leaned forward. Disrespect never came easy for me, but I would not let him out of this. "I think you have the explaining to do. Why didn't you tell me about Uncle Carl and his family?"

His shoulders seemed to fold forward as if he had been drained of all energy. "Michael," he sighed, "Your uncle was my younger brother. I was always doing things for him. When we were little, I did his chores just because it was easier than having my poor mother yell at him. I guess I carried that through life. I got him job after job. Finally, he seemed to be happy working at the factory. He struggled, but he and Julie, she was your aunt, they seemed happy. They loved their children." He looked to me with eyes so full of anguish I wanted him to stop, but I didn't dare ask. "I got busy with the paper. I was just like you," he forced a smile. "I loved the scent of a good story. I was always on the beat. I got the byline. I got the picture. I was the best at building news when in actuality there was no news at all." I took exception at his comparison to me, but I said nothing. "News was my life. My brother, his family and even your mother played second fiddle. The day Carl killed his family and turned the gun on him self, I was on my way to cover a real story. I sensed the blood and the gore. I was sounding the words over and over in my head. I had the story almost written." He leaned back and closed his eyes tightly. "Do you know that I was so consumed with the story, that I didn't even realize that the address I was given was Carl's home?"

I swallowed hard. How many stories consumed my attention while my dad struggled alone at home?

"Michael, if you learned one thing in Detroit, I hope it was that your family and friends are really what counts."

I received my chastisement with grace, but I could not look at my father, not with my deceit on my lips. "I'm home, aren't I?"

"That article, I never wanted to see it again. It showed me more about myself that I ever wanted to see. It showed me what I became. There I was. I was mourning, and my own paper dared to intrude on my grief. I buried my brother and his family. I packed up what I owned, and with the little bit of savings your mother and I managed to put away, we settled here."

"I understand."

"I don't think you can. You still want the big byline. You're bored here. Don't think I can't tell."

"It's just taking a while, Dad, but I'm growing used to it."

"I want you to burn that article. I don't ever want to see it again. It drudges up too much of the past."

"I'll take care of it." I picked up our plates and quickly washed the dishes so he would not have to worry about it. When I finished, I found him already asleep in his chair, the television on low. I picked up the article. He would never see it again, but I planned to keep it, if only to remember the lesson my father just taught me. He was right. Friends and family were too important to be lost to a cruel world. Then I remembered there was someone I needed to see.

⋗ ✝ ⋖

Jake mentioned that Seth no longer lived in his home on Second Avenue, an older Serenity Key homestead left to him by his maternal grandparents. As I walked down the street, I enjoyed the lights and the trees in the window. I was reminded of the celebration I recently shared with the Williams' family. Seth's home was the only one completely dark. There was a pile of trash in the front for the garbage workers, and it appeared that Seth may have relented a little and cleaned the abandoned house. I don't know how it caught my eyes, but I saw it lying in the trash in front of Seth's home. The verse was wrinkled and torn. I had to walk into the brightly lit yard of Seth's neighbor to read it. "Thou, therefore, my son, be strong in the grace that is in Christ Jesus. II Timothy 2:1." I held the angel. Her body and wings were crushed but otherwise she was fine. I carried it with me toward Seth's second home.

I found him sitting on the deck of his boat. He held a bottle of Jim Beam whiskey in his hand. I noticed immediately that it was unopened and that he was not alone. Jesse sat beside him. Both were staring up into the night sky studying the stars until they felt my presence. Seth was the first to look toward me. He turned his lips into a forced smile. "Welcome home, Michael." He did not bother to stand but tipped the bottle in my direction motioning for me to join them.

"Good to be home. I'm sorry I haven't been by before, but the paper has kept me busy." I sat in a lawn chair opposite the two men. "I was so sorry to hear about your wife."

Seth nodded, "You didn't know her, did you?"

I shook my head. "You met and married after I left Serenity. Mickey wrote me about your marriage, and I was surprised it wasn't ...." I caught a definite nod from Jesse that told me not to mention the name of the lovely blonde. "I was surprised, but I've heard a lot about the woman you married. Linda was apparently well loved."

"Hey, she could stand Seth. She was unbelievable," Jesse tried to lighten the mood. Silence fell between us then and I knew I was interrupting a serious conversation between the two men.

"Am I — Should I come back some other time?"
Seth shook his head. "What's that in your hand?" He asked.

I hesitated and Jesse's eyes grew large. He shook his head, trying to warn me off this subject as well. As I brought the angel forward, he bit his lip. "I believe it belongs to you," I spoke to our friend.

Seth squinted to see in the semi-darkness. "Nope," he nodded. "It belongs to my trash."

He was so hard and cynical. He was just as I imagined myself to be while living in Detroit, but I realized I was not so well affected by life as I believed. I still held hope and love inside of me. "Are you planning on drinking that?" I asked the two men.

"No," Seth shook his head once again. "No. It's just sitting here like an old friend. I was lonely, and look, two of my older friends showed up to keep me company," he eyed Jesse as if they were sharing a joke at my expense. I could tell that Jesse was not amused. "Friends, good friends." The words were sarcastic, and they were directed at me.

"I'm here now, Seth. You are a good friend to me."

"We're here, too," the voice came from the dock and we turned to see Mickey helping Sandy onto the boat. Sandy turned and looked back into the darkness. "Hurry up," she demanded.

"We're coming," Blanchie suddenly came into view alone. I helped her onto the boat wondering who the "we" happened to be. With Blanchie, one might assume a very large invisible white rabbit was following her. It was nervousness that caused the thought to float through my mind, and I smiled at her as she curtsied in response to my politeness.

"What is this, a show?" Seth's sharp words ended my amusement.

"We saw Michael heading your way, and we thought we would join him," Sandy explained. I knew it was a half-truth. Somewhere down the line someone had watched me walk in this direction and that person called everyone together. Whatever the case, I knew I was to be the spokesman. Seth stood. He swung the bottle with all his might. It hit a wood piling toward the back of the boat, shattered and fell into the water. The movement startled Blanchie, and she fell against me. I steadied her with my arm around her shoulder. "I don't need any of you," Seth barked.

"What do you need?" Blanchie pulled from me. "You're in trouble, Seth, and you're too lost in your self-pity to know it." For such a small woman, she suddenly brought courage to the rest of us. We stood like protection from evil around our friend. It was unspoken, but we all agreed that we were not going to move until Seth was safe. As if on cue, Jesse stood beside Blanchie and the wall of four grew a little larger. I thought of Turk's view of the angels. We formed a wall of protection.

"I need a good woman to love me and care for me. Oops, I had that, and God just took her away. I don't need an angel to remind me of what I lost."

"I think the angel is to remind you that you're not alone. Jesus is with you," Blanchie stated in her simplicity.

"He's left the building!" Seth screamed. "He left me when he took my life away from me. He took so much away from me, too much, more than any of you know."

I saw her approaching the dock, and I thanked God that she could not hear his words. She stood in the distance watching, not hearing. She was the other half of Blanchie's "we". She was beautiful, and Seth was ignorant in his grief if he did not realize how much of his life he retained.

I always knew that Hannah Miller had a look about her, an ethereal quality that set her apart from other girls. The inability to hear only added to that contrast. Her large blue eyes never left Seth.

"You're life wasn't taken away," Mickey reasoned. "It was changed. It was made different. You encountered sadness, grief. We've all been there. All of us here, everyone of us are suffering."

"Suffering? What do any of you know about suffering? I can write a book on it. I can spell it out for you. It's a living death. I have nothing to live for, nothing to sustain me."

"You're suffering at your own hand," I blurted. "You're leaning on a crutch because you don't want to go on and live like your wife would have wanted you to do. When she was dying, Seth, did she tell you to give up and die after her?"

"My mother isn't saying that," Mickey spoke. "She's telling me to live and to do everything I ever dreamed of doing. I watch her dying everyday, and she's suffering, Seth. She wants to go home to be with God, but she's torn between her family and Him. I'm suffering watching her, but once she's gone, I plan to go on with my life and show the world her contribution. Momma won't be suffering and Linda isn't suffering any more."

"Suffering comes in different forms," Jesse looked at Blanchie beside him. "I'm suffering at my own hands, too. I'm making Blanchie suffer through it also." He tried hard to contain his emotions. "Michael's right. We're using a crutch. I keep telling myself I need to suffer, but I don't need to, do I? The divorce was final today, and I need to go on."

Blanchie nodded her agreement. Otherwise, she did not move, and I knew it was the hardest thing she had ever done. "I love you," she whispered, and I was not sure if Jesse could hear.

"I love you," he answered. "And I understand. Someday...."

"That's just it. I don't have a someday!" Seth screamed. "My someday is over!"

Because the girl on the dock could see his anguish, I tried to calm him. "Seth, Hannah is here, and if anyone can tell you about suffering, I think she can."

Seth whirled around. His look was long and hard at the blonde who stood close to the edge of darkness. When he turned back to me, he looked defeated, worn, and used by life. He was no longer sustained by his self-pity. He reached out for the object in my hand. "Why'd you put it in the trash?" I asked as I handed it to him.

"It's not real," he shrugged.

"But the person who made it for you obviously cares. That person is real."

"I don't need an angel to tell me about the grace of Jesus Christ. He's graced me abundantly." His voice was again edged with hardness. "He gave me all the loneliness and sadness I could ever hope to have. He left a hole in my heart that I cannot fill."

I did feel sorry for him, but I knew not to show it. His friends surrounded him now, and we did not need to show pity. He had enough of that for himself. I reached out and took the delicate rose angel back from him. I held it up. "So what?" I nodded my head toward Hannah. "Your wife died. Does that mean that you close your eyes to all the good things that are left? You have a job I know you love. You have a father who loves you. You have people around you who may be slow in showing you, but we care about you very much. Most importantly, you have always carried Hannah's heart with you whether you've known it or not." Seth looked to the blonde. It had not escaped me that the skirt and blouse the woman wore were of the same rose as the angel. "I ran from a little girl once, and she never forgave me. You've bypassed Hannah's friendship for so long that it's a wonder she still cares as much for you as she does."

Mickey stepped back onto the dock. Hannah came toward him, and he helped her aboard. He kissed her cheek, and spoke silently so that only she could read his lips. She nodded her understanding and moved past us to stand directly in front of Seth. "You are my best friend," she signed. "I love you." It was apparently the first time she ever admitted to him what was so obvious to anyone who ever saw them together. Although Seth reached out for the lifeline Hannah tossed, it was clear he did not understand the depth of the love she proclaimed. "I will stand by you no matter what you think of me, but you must wake up and start living." Her voice was the thick sound of the deaf, but her words were clear even as he enfolded her in his arms and sobbed against her. "I love you," she repeated.

"Hold me so I know you're real. You're my angel, Hannah. That thing, that lifeless thing, can't compare to the compassion you showed to me and to Linda." Although Hannah could not hear a word he was saying nor could she read his lips, she could feel his anguish as he cried against her.

Jesse placed his hand on my shoulder. "I thought we were goners when you showed him that thing." He playfully wiped his brow; the scene from a few minutes earlier was forgotten. Blanchie hugged her sister to her, and Mickey stepped over beside Jesse and I.

"Thank you," Seth composed himself. "I'm sorry if I said anything to hurt any of you. I don't always act like it, but you guys are important to me."

"Ah," Mickey winked, "Nothing we won't forgive over a period of two or three years." He smiled at me, and I enjoyed his joke.

Seth took the angel once again from my hand. "Did it make you angry?" My newsman curiosity came through.

"Michael," Jesse warned playfully, "Let it alone."

"This thing," Seth handed it to the girl he still held in his arm. "Yeah, well, not it, the card."

"Where did it come from?"

"It was on my table below," he advised. "Someone left it. I figured it was Hannah. She's always harping at me about God's love and Jesus' grace."

"Have you ever thought of angels?" I asked.

Seth nodded, "Not much."

"Give me an idea of what you believe about angels, Seth."

The man before me couldn't speak for a long while. He would start, but emotion would overcome him and he would pause. Finally, he looked up at me. "I think all angels look like Hannah with long blonde hair and big blue eyes." He stopped to recover his emotions again. "Angels are supposed to comfort us, aren't they?" He was asking me, the most unqualified to answer.

"I'm finding they may have a lot of duties," I gave him the benefit of my limited knowledge. "And some of us keep them busier than others." I remembered my mother's belief about Jesse's special guardian.

"Yeah," Seth chuckled then grew somber. "I'm angry with God." His teeth were clenched. "So, I don't need his angels."

His words mirrored much of my thoughts after the loss of my mother. "I've been angry with Him, too," I admitted. I had not realized until that very moment how much my heart had softened. For so long I held silent. No one ever knew that I blamed God for my mother's death. As I spoke to my friend, I can honestly say that all anger was gone.

"Pop told me that Trevor's still feeling pretty lousy. How does he seem to you?"

"Weak."

The anger left Seth completely. It was replaced by concern for my father. "He'll come around. He needs some rest."

I simply nodded, "Why don't you stop by and say hello. He'd enjoy a visit from you."

"I will," he told me. "I guess you'll cover the council meeting. Go easy on me."

"We're with you." It was Mickey. "You just need to pick yourself up and go on. If you can promise that, we'll be behind you all the way."

Seth pulled Hannah closer to him. "That's what Hannah's been telling me all along." He touched the angel Hannah held in her hand. "Mind if I keep this?" He asked.

"It's yours." I told him. "And I believe the verse speaks to all of us." One by one we left Seth and Hannah alone and walked silently off the dock into the darkness. Without words we each went our own separate way, but I know that our minds were filled with the same thoughts. Even in turmoil, God's grace was boundless.

Chapter Seven

Sweet Release

"That Christ may dwell in your hearts by faith; that ye, being rooted and grounded in love, may be able to comprehend with all saints what is the breadth, and length, and depth, and height; and to know the love of Christ, which passeth knowledge, that ye might be filled with all the fullness of God." - Ephesians 3:17-19.

After leaving Seth, I worked alone at the *Serenade* on the story that engulfed my life and affected me deeply. When I exhausted myself on the subject, I put the writing away and printed the current week's paper. I felt pride with my accomplishment as I handed the first copy to my father over breakfast. He read it slowly as I sat and waited for his critique. "I'm leaving my work in very capable hands," he finally laid the paper aside.

Those were not the words I expected to hear, and I straightened as if slapped. "Are you planning to leave?"

"I'm tired," his shoulders seemed to sag. "Each day is a struggle."

"Life shouldn't be hard. It's made that way by unhappiness," I remembered the very words he spoke to me a lifetime ago, my mother's words. "Are you unhappy?"

"It has nothing to do with unhappiness, Michael."

"It has to do with giving up, and you only do that when you have no hope. What's the difference now? Did you feel this way when you lost your brother? What about when we lost Mom? Where did your hope go, Dad?"

He took a haggard breath. "Hope is all I have. I hope that my body stays as strong as my mind, but it ebbs away daily. Truth is it's taking my mind with it. Each day, I lose a little more of the sharpness. Why do you think I stopped writing? I gave it up because I just don't have what it takes?"

"I can't accept that. I won't accept it." I stared at him, but he did not respond. I wanted to fight. I wanted to pull the truth out of him the way he demanded it from me that night so long ago when he offered me the freedom to leave home and chase my dreams. He was unhappy, and he didn't seem to want to live, and I wanted to know why. When he remained silent, my anger grew, and I knew it was best for me to leave before I said something to add to his unhappiness. "I'm going to deliver the paper." I heard him yell that the paper was a day early, but I allowed the slamming door to stand as my answer.

I was furious with him for giving up. I was angry at Valley for giving in, and I was angry with myself for caring at all. For the first time since I arrived in Serenity Key, I was ready to return to Detroit where I did not let myself feel. I wanted to cover real stories about people that I didn't love or want to protect. I wanted to forget about make-believe angels. I loaded the old truck and started off for town, leaving bundles at every usual stop.

The papers delivered, I knew there was one stop I had to make. I pulled the truck up in front of the Roberts' home. I remembered my failure to pay Mickey for his contribution, and I convinced myself that subconsciously I wanted to make that right. I knocked and Sandy answered. Her hair was uncombed, and her eyes were red from lack of sleep and recently shed tears. "She's bad today," she proclaimed.

"I wanted to visit. I promised her I would." I did not realize until that moment how badly I wanted to see Sabrina Roberts. In my hand I held the paper and the article written by her son especially for her. Mickey wanted to give her a gift that only he could offer. Sandy motioned me upstairs. I knocked as I entered the room. Valley and Mickey sat on each side of Sabrina, each holding her hand. It was Valley who moved aside. "Momma, Michael's here to see you," she was only too glad to give me her seat.

Sabrina Roberts opened her eyes. She held her feeble hand up for a moment and let it fall back upon the bed. "I have the paper," I told her. "It's hot off the press and a day early. Maybe Mickey could read it to you."

"You," she said softly. Mickey, I noticed, never lifted his head to acknowledge me.

I opened the pages to exactly where I wanted to start. "Momma's Gift by Michael Roberts, Jr." Sabrina lifted her eyes just a bit, but she was too weak to show much else in the way of surprise.

"It was my mother that taught my sister and me the real worth of Christmas. It came not in the presents under the tree or from the cakes and cookies in the oven. The treasure of Christmas came from the light that shined within Sabrina Roberts. It was her love for Jesus Christ that she shared so openly. That is what made this Holiday so very special. I remember telling my mother that I heard once that Christmas had no value any longer. I told her that even the Lord's name had been taken away from the day itself, replaced by a simple "X". A smile graced her face so serene, so at peace. She pushed my hair from my face, and said simply, 'If someone believes that, Michael, they're not looking in the right place.' With those words my mother placed her hand over my heart. 'No one can take Him from us," she kissed my face. 'No one, nothing.'

"My mother received a special gift recently. It bore a verse, her favorite. In this verse Paul confirms exactly what she tried to teach me that day. Nothing can separate us from the love of Christ Jesus. Momma rests in that verse day and night, and she wants more than anything to tell the bearer of the gift thank you. Momma has forgotten that the present she received was not from just anyone. The thought came from a friend, a very special friend to think of her at this time in her life, but the words came to her from the Lord for such a time as this. They are to my mother, encouragement, hope and love, all the wonderful things our mother has always been to her family and friends.

"There is no tree in our home this Christmas. The house sits dark. Still, we rejoice in awesome wonder. Even in sadness, Christmas is not devalued in our hearts. You see, Momma's ready to venture home where praises for the reason we celebrate the season are sung on high. Heaven's doors are open. The lights are bright there. The "X" is removed and Christ stands in His place. His worth is declared far beyond priceless. He is waiting for Sabrina Roberts. It is in His time that she will take the short journey into His arms. No longer will Christ simply be in her heart but He will be at hand. He knows when Sabrina Roberts is to enter, when she will leave her pain far behind.

"Momma will always be in our hearts, and we will rejoice in what she has taught us. She worked hard to show us Christ in her, and when we stepped away from His love, it was Momma that reminded us that we could always turn to Him in our times of need. We want Momma to know that she will not be leaving her children alone. She has introduced us to Christ, and He will remain with us. She will also leave enough of her own love to sustain us until we see her again.

"Each year we asked Momma what she wanted for Christmas, and each year the answer was the same. She told us that all she wanted was to know that she would see us in Heaven and that we would be together in Glory. This year I discussed Momma's request with my sister. We'll be there, Momma, but it's not a gift we could ever offer. It is Christ's special gift to you borne from His love. Merry Christmas, Sabrina."

As I folded the paper and looked up, Mickey's body was trembling. Sandy stood beside him, holding his shoulders tightly. Valley appeared to have stopped breathing. When I looked to Sabrina, she was at peace, a smile on her face, but she was gone. I lowered my head. "You gave her the greatest gift of all, Mickey. You gave her permission to leave."

"It was the hardest thing to do," he stood with great effort. "I'll call Seth and Curt."

He left the room to notify the police chief and the emergency technician who would record Sabrina's death. An ambulance would also be called to carry Sabrina away.

Valley remained unmoving. There was no visible emotion. Sandy moved toward her, and she backed away. I laid the paper down. "Valley, sit."

She blinked as if to clear her mind. "She's gone. She's gone." Her voice was low. She was on the verge of hysteria. She moved to the bedside again. "Momma! No. Momma!" She screamed.

Mickey ran back into the room. He struggled with her until she allowed him to hold her close. "She's gone from here, Valley, that's all," he soothed. "She's gone home," he brushed her hair. Sandy moved past them.

"I have no one," Valley cried against her brother.

"You have me, Sissy. You have me," he continued to calm her. I walked from the room. As I headed down the hall, I looked into Sandy and Mickey's room. Sandy sat on the bed, her face covered by her hands. Her body was shaking with emotions that needed to be spent. I moved slowly down the stairs. Tears also stung my eyes. I would miss the strong woman that suffered so much in the end. I made it down the stairs and out onto the porch. "Michael!" The screen door slammed open. I turned to face Valley but instead felt her thin body fall against mine. "I'm sorry. I'm sorry," she cried. I brushed her auburn hair with a kiss, held her. "Nothing to be sorry about."

She pulled from me, "When I left here before I should have told you I was going."

I stared at her not wanting to know where this was headed.

"I wanted to tell you this time," she wiped her tears. "Momma's gone. I'm going back to Detroit as soon as I can."

I could only nod. Were her words meant to tear at my heart, or was she simply blind to the pain she was causing?

"Brad needs me," she placed her hand against her stomach. "We're having a baby."

I held up my hand to silence her. Her proclamation suddenly made me understand that what I had been doing was very, very wrong.

"It's just that..."

"I've heard it all before."

"I've never told you."

"I have covered enough stories on battered and abused women that I know the story by heart. I heard you tell it to me in the hospital, and I don't need it repeated here. Please take care of your child better than you do yourself."

"You'll be going back?" It was a question.

I did not answer her.

"I mean, you'll be there as soon as ...."

"As soon as what?" I refused to believe that life had left her so unfeeling. She suspected my father was not well. She knew I would not leave until he no longer needed me. I looked into her blue eyes, and suddenly I knew. She had always been that way. It should have been obvious to me. She didn't want to be with her mother when Sabrina needed her daughter the most. She left Sandy to be a surrogate. Each time her mother needed her it was Mickey that made Valley return. She would not be home now without my intervention.

"As soon as you're not needed here any longer," her look was hopeful.

I took a deep breath. "What would it matter if I were in Detroit or here on Serenity? When you leave this place, when you walk out on your brother and Sandy and you return to that scum you call a husband, that will be the end of anything that you and I ever had." I shook my head reminding myself of my new discovery. Valley wasn't all to blame. "We never did have anything." I admitted.

"Friends. Weren't we always friends?"

Again I shook my head. "I thought that one time, but now I think you're no more capable of friendship than you are love." I saw my best friend standing in the screen door, and I was sorry for the truth he was forced to hear. "Valley, if you go back to Brad now, you're an idiot. At least wait until he has some counseling. You need counseling. The way you two are living, it's not right. It's a warped view of life. You're placing the baby in danger."

"How dare you..."

"I'll tell you how I dare. I love you. I love you with all my heart and my soul. I've tried to deny that for years now. Today, for the first time, I remembered you're another man's wife, and I have no right to feel the way I do about you. It's wrong. I've tried to forget you. I buried myself in my work, and I told myself that you knew what you were doing. I almost convinced myself that I was over you. Then I run into you in an emergency room. Your face is black and blue and your lip is cut, and I learn that the man you married doesn't respect the vows you made to each other any more that I have. I was ready to leave everything I had in Detroit to bring you back to Serenity and keep you safe from harm to show you over time that friendship and love are very different than you've been taught by Brad, and you told me that wasn't what you wanted. You wanted to remain with the animal that is more than likely going to take you permanently away from all of us. You hurt me, Valley, because you're hurting yourself. If you and Brad love each other, for God's sake get help so you can show that love in the right way." I fought to stand where I was, to keep from taking her shoulders in my grip and shaking sense into her.

"I make up my own mind. I can do what I want."

"Then prove it. Stay here and make Brad meet you on equal ground. Hasn't he alienated you enough? Haven't we proven to you that he's been filling your head full of doubts and lies?"

"Do you still love me?" The question came out of left field, and I was confused by it.

Against my will, my head nodded, providing her with the answer she wanted. "Love isn't anything I throw around lightly."

"And if I stayed, you'd take care of me?"

"Is that what you want?" Mickey started to open the door. I shook my head in warning and he remained on the porch.

"Would you?" She demanded an answer from me.

"After you proved you could take care of yourself, if you wanted to start with friendship and let what could happen —— Right now, you're another man's wife, and you say you're carrying his child. I will not promise you more than friendship."

"But you just said I wasn't capable of friendship or love," her tone was mocking, self righteous. She was good. She had learned well. She was picking the fight. She was pushing me to my limits. It was all too classic, all right in line with the information I gleaned for my articles in Detroit. She wanted me to prove my love to her, and to prove it, in her mind, I had to strike out, to verbally abuse her or to physically lay my hands on her. I loved her too much. I could not play the game. I needed to let her go. There was nothing else to do.

"I'm sorry about your mother, Valley. I hope that after it all settles in, you can find peace with yourself. I know you're heading back to Detroit," I started toward her to kiss her cheek. She backed away, fear in her eyes. I stopped. "Don't look me up in Detroit unless you and Brad have gotten some help. Then, if you call me to tell me you're leaving him, I'll have Mickey there in two minutes, whether I'm still here or I'm back there." The words were meant to cut the ties, at least for me.

"I won't need you. You're not half the man Brad Rasneck is. I despise all of you. Mickey makes me come back here to watch Momma die. I didn't want to see her die. Why did I want to go through that? He could have just called me to let me know."

"It wasn't for you," Mickey stepped off the porch onto the lower step. I brought you back for Momma. Can't you understand that? Momma needed to see you. She needed that peace of mind. It was as important for her to see you as it was for her to be assured of our salvation."

Valley pushed past him and stormed into the house. Mickey stepped down beside me. "Do you think she'll ever come around?"

"I don't know. She needs counseling."

"So you told her," a tense smile formed. "I'm glad it came out. You can put it behind you now."

"I don't think I'll ever put your sister behind me. I care a lot about her." I moved after him, and we both sat together on the porch steps like we had done many times before.

"We sat here after Dad's funeral," Mickey's thoughts were the same as mine. "I felt him here," he brushed a piece of lint off his jeans leg. "I was praying that Jesus would send him to take her home," he bit his lip to control his emotions before going on. "And while you were reading, I —- You know how sometimes a breeze will blow, or there will be a certain sound, and you remember something or someone so strongly."

I nodded. There were times when my own mother seemed to be beside me. I couldn't explain it.

"I swear I smelled Old Spice. It was what Dad wore. Every once in a while something will happen, and I'll recall that scent, and I could swear that he's with me. It was like that today. You were reading, and from nowhere there it was."

"Your mother wouldn't be happy if you said you believed in ghosts," I reminded him.

"What else could it be, Michael? Right then, I knew Momma was gone. She went with him."

"I can't begin to explain it," I was honest with him, "But it must have been some comfort to you."

He nodded. "It was," he wiped his eyes. Despite his effort, tears ran down his cheek. He coughed and sobbed for sometime while I sat with him. The fire truck and the police car pulled up in front of the house, and it wasn't long afterward that the ambulance from the mainland arrived. Our friends patted Mickey's back. Curt bent down. "I called Pastor Crum," he spoke softly. "He's on his way." Mickey's only answer was a nod. Curt followed after Seth.

After a few moments, Mickey turned his face toward me. "I wrote the words I did to release my mother, Michael," his face showed the obvious strain of trying once again to hide his emotions. "You need to take the actions of her only daughter to heart and release those feelings that bind you to her. Let her go."

I hugged him to me. We were more than friends. He was my brother. Our bond was closer than any bond he and his sister ever held because we were so much alike. "Love you, Man," together we let emotions show that would have embarrassed us had we been young boys again.

Chapter Eight

Angels Abound

"And I John saw these things, and heard them. And when I
had heard and seen, I fell down to worship before the feet
of the angel which shewed me these things. Then saith he
unto me, See thou do it not: for I am thy fellow-servant,
and of thy brethren the prophets, and of them which keep
the sayings of this book: worship God." - Revelation 22: 8-9.

*T*he week before Christmas was hectic, but in the midst of the hus-
tle, Serenity Key came to a standstill as many of its residents attended
the funeral of Sabrina Roberts. My father was dressed in the same suit
he wore to his own wife's funeral a few years before. We sat together
with Seth New who would later be addressing the town council con-
cerning his ability to perform the duties for which he had been
entrusted. Seth was obviously uncomfortable as Melvin Crum spoke
of the comfort that Jesus can offer in times of great loss. I watched as
his hands curled to grip the soft cushion of the pew. I knew that my
friend, for whatever reason, felt a great deal of anger at the Lord, and
I suspected it had to do with more than the loss of his wife. When
Seth looked to me, his eyes were filled with tears. "Give it to Him,
Seth. He'll listen," I whispered.

"I'd like to give it to Him." Seth's voice held all the anger you could
see in his continued grip on the pew cushion, but he remained
through the service. There had been a change in our friend since the
night a few days before when we met on his boat. Jesse mentioned it.

Mickey commented on it. He no longer drank, and Jesse advised he and Hannah were seen throwing out bottles and cans of alcohol. He cleaned himself up considerably, and his hair was trimmed and neat. His eyes were no longer glassed over by the booze. Still, he was wrestling with God, and there was no doubt in my mind about the outcome of the match. I just wondered how long God would take to pin my buddy to the mat.

After Sabrina's funeral, it seemed the entire town met at the Roberts' house. The food started coming soon after the arrival of the fire truck and ambulance the day of Sabrina's death. Now, it was set from one end of the dining table to the other and everyone gathered in tiny groups. Sally and Turk Williams eventually joined my father and I. It wasn't long before Curt Davis and Seth drew near. "That was some story Mickey wrote," Sally Williams commented. "It broke my heart."

"They need a tree," Turk declared. "I can't see them not having a tree." He left us, pushing open the front door before I could stop him.

"Let him go," Sally Williams touched my arm. "He's a big man with a big heart, and he doesn't always know how to say the right words. The tree is his way of saying he cares." She turned her attention to Seth brushing her fingers over his shirt collar as if he were a child, and she his mother. "We'll be at the meeting tonight," she told him. "We plan to support you." It occurred to me suddenly that the words I heard since my youth were very true. When the Lord takes, he also gives back tenfold. The Lord had given us Sally Williams as an encourager to replace Sabrina whom he had taken home.

"Thank you," Seth nodded. "Curt said the same thing."

"We'll all be there," I assured.

"I do appreciate it," he was uncomfortable. "But whatever happens, I know that I've made my own bed. No one is responsible for what has happened to me. I did it all myself."

Searching the room, I saw a familiar face. She was standing alone looking about her as if someone were about to sneak up from behind. I smiled, and she waved politely. I left our little circle and moved to where she stood.

Bella Edwards was a beautiful girl with eyes of emerald green and hair of the darkest chocolate. It bounced around her shoulders in thick waves. Her smile was genuine and immediately made you feel comfortable in her presence. I had not talked to her at all since my return, and as I faced her, I was all too well aware that there were whispers in the room, stares directed her way, and I knew that she could feel it also. "How have you been?" I asked.

"I've been well."

"And your Aunt Rosa and Uncle Ed?"

She looked down at her black high heels and back to me. Her lips were no longer turned into a gracious smile. "They're doing fine."

"I saw Noah earlier. Is he around?"

She nodded, "He had to leave with Pastor Crum. He'll be back in a minute."

I could not resist. I knew that no one had bothered to ask her, and my newsman's curiosity was tugging at me. "Everything okay between the two of you?"

Her smile that had vanished returned. "We're just fine." I knew she was telling the truth.

"So, when's the wedding?"

"February 14th." Her face glowed with happiness.

"Bella, I spoke with Curt."

The smile vanished once again. Her eyes darted to Curt who was still standing where I left him seconds earlier. "Curty told you?"

I immediately sensed a misunderstanding. We were going in a direction I was sure she did not want to take. "About the angel Noah received?"

She laughed softly, "Oh." The sigh of relief was too obvious. "It's the most beautiful gift anyone has ever given us."

"I thought it was left for Noah?"

"It was," she glowed. "But it spoke to both of us. It saved us from making an awful mistake."

"I believe I know a little about that, too," I could not pretend to be completely ignorant. It wasn't fair to Bella. In that, I recognized my journalistic prowess had lessened since my return from Detroit. "Curt mentioned that there's a misunderstanding between you and Noah." Bella shifted uneasily, and I placed my hand on her shoulder. "I believe him when he says that you've been faithful to Noah."

"I haven't done anything," she searched for the tissues she carried in her purse. "Aunt Rosa, she's —- I don't know why she's said these horrible things. Curty and I —- I love Curty, but it's not like that. I can't explain it to anyone. I can't deny my love for Curt because —- No one would understand what he is to me, what he's done for me. I can't even tell Noah, but ..." She struggled to remain calm all the while trying to find the elusive tissues. I pulled my handkerchief from my back pocket and she took it gratefully. "Noah has been so wonderful. He accepts my privacy, and he has faith in me." Tears ran down her face, and she wiped them away. People were beginning to stare.

"Are you okay?" Curt rushed over to us. "Bella?"

She nodded without looking to the man. Curt was not helping the situation. A low murmur filled the house. "Pastor Crum and Noah are finalizing plans," she managed to say.

"Your marriage?"

She shook her head. "Melvin is going into the missionary field. Noah has been asked to replace him as pastor."

"That's great," I said.

"That isn't what you want, is it Bella?" Curt questioned.

She looked up to the man who stood by my side. "It's what the Lord wants, Curty. I know that Noah and I were planning to ask Melvin if he would petition the church to send us out as missionaries, but when we went to Melvin, he was so happy. He was ready for a change. He felt the Lord calling him to mission work." Another small laugh sounded through her tears. "I saw how happy Noah was at the news, and I knew that the Lord has other plans for us. My unhappiness here was causing me to push Noah away from Serenity." Her slender fingers touched my arm. "That angel, it was an inspirational gift. It's verse spoke to Noah in one way and to me in another."

"What do you mean?" I asked.

"Hebrews 11:1, Now faith is the substance of things hoped for, the evidence of things not seen," Noah McGowan stepped into our small circle. Just as soon, Curt Davis moved away. Noah's gaze followed him, and once Curt rejoined Sally, his eyes met Noah's for a brief second. I felt a deep sadness for the two men. They had been friends much of their lives, and it was something as simple as a secret that kept them apart. By instinct, I looked to where my friend stood in conversation with Jake New. Mickey offered me a smile, and I returned my attention to the soon-to-be pastor and his soon-to-be bride.

"What did the angel mean to you?" I asked Noah. After all, he was the most qualified to answer.

Noah's arm went protectively around his fiancé. "I know what it was meant to say to me, but it spoke that to Bella. What it told me is that I needed to trust the woman I love and stand beside her. In the end, no matter how long it takes, I'll be rewarded for my faith."

"Faith in Bella?" I was confused.

"Faith in God's will in Bella's life and in my life."

"And what did you take from the verse?" I asked the beautiful woman by his side.

"What I told you earlier. I realized that Noah wasn't really convinced that we should go into mission work. We have prayed about it and prayed about it for years. My heart was broken when I realized that God didn't intend for us to go into that work, at least right now." She smiled at Noah. "I mean, Michael, Noah and I have grown up next door to each other and right across the street from where we live is the church we attended all of our lives. We grew up attending that church on Sunday mornings, Sunday nights, Wednesday nights and any other night there was a service or a fellowship. God has never let us wander from him. Noah and I have loved God, and we have loved each other forever. Since we were sixteen we've planned our marriage in that church," tears sprang to her eyes again. "And when Melvin Crum mentioned that he wanted to leave his position the day after we were married, I understood that God has always known where we would be on February 15th."

It was a powerful statement of faith. I wasn't sure of all of the undercurrents around Noah and Bella, but I recognized that some could have been strong enough to tear their love apart. They stood before me confirming their love for each other and God's love toward them. "I hope," I said, emotion tearing at my heart, "I truly hope that when I find the right woman to love, it will be a bond as strong as yours."

"That can only happen if you make Jesus the center of everything you do," Noah preached.

"I wish the two of you all the happiness in the world," I started to walk away.

"Wait a minute," Noah caught my attention. I turned back. "Sandy told us you always ask one important question," he pulled the angel from his pocket. It was yellow, the same color as the angel Turk Williams received. "Do you care to hear my humble opinion?" I nodded as if a denial would stop Noah McGowan. "Angels sent by God are messengers," he said plainly. "But when Jesus appears as an angel, he appears as a deliverer, a protector, an encourager, and a comforter." He came close to me. His words were low, and well intended. "Don't make these tatted angels into something they aren't. They are gifts from a very nice person. Angels are not meant for worship, that belongs to God."

＊ ✝ ＊

It was two hours later when the crowd left. My father rested comfortably in the living room while Sally, Seth, Curt and I helped the Roberts clean up. From the kitchen we heard the deep, "Ho, Ho, Ho." Looking one to the other, we moved toward the living room. Laughter filled the air as Turk stood in the doorway, a large tree in front of him hiding the full view of his Santa suit. He marched forward and put the tree down. "Santa forgot to ask you if you have a tree stand." He hinted, and although it took a few moments, a stand was presented. Mickey and Sandy seemed to enjoy their respite from grief. They were alone as a family. Valley true to her word left Serenity before her mother's funeral. I tried not to think of her, but I knew she was not far from Mickey's thoughts either.

With the tree decorated, Dad and I left. He was tired and went for a nap right away. I went to the office. Word had gotten around that I was inquiring about the angels, and calls had been received. I took detailed notes from each individual, separating the angels by cause and then, curiosity gaining the upper hand, by color. Amazingly, I saw a trend. Blue angels were meant to comfort the dying. I was thankful there were only two. Over the last several years there had been too many deaths in Serenity. The rose colored angels were given to people coping with loss. Mickey received one shortly after Sabrina's death. It was similar to the one given to Seth. Mickey's angel held not one verse but the entire 23rd Psalm.

Yellow angels seemed reserved for life changing events, Turk's angel because he survived a shooting and Noah McGowan because he graduated seminary and was embarking on God's calling. Several other yellow angels seemed to arrive with the birth of children. Green seemed to be given for growth, moving on, making decisions. Blanchie and Jesse both had to grow, to decide, to make tough decisions. They remained divorced, although Jesse seemed to be staying out of trouble and a little closer to his cabin in the woods. Melvin Crum, Jesse's father, received a yellow angel with the announcement that he would be leaving the Serenity Key Baptist Church in Noah McGowan's capable hands, and he would be leaving for the mission field. Jesse related to me that he felt that his father was following in Blanchie's footsteps. He was leaving and taking Jesse's last haven of refuge. I did mention to Jesse that his father had never done anything in life without a lot of prayer and full conviction that it was the Lord's will. Jesse agreed and smiled as he declared it a conspiracy of major proportions.

The meaning of one angel remained unsolved. No other angel like it had been received. It was a symbol unto itself. Its verse was the only one that seemed not meant for any occasion. Its color, bolder than all others, set it apart. It sat in front of me on my desk as I wrote. My mind reviewed the verse over and over again, but it never became clear to me. It didn't matter that I couldn't comprehend the verse. The angel was meant for my father, and I couldn't understand why the verse offered him no comfort.

It was Georgie that reminded me of the council meeting. He stayed underfoot seldom lately. My father kept him busy with errands leaving me to attend to the family business.

"You'll stand up for Mr. Seth?" Georgie inquired.

"Yes, Georgie," I assured. "If I'm asked, I'll speak for him."

"Good. He needs you. He likes you a lot, you know. He told me. He said you were a good man to have in his corner."

I placed a hand on his broad shoulder. "I've said the same thing about you. What would we do without you?"

"I'll never leave." He told me. "But you will. You'll go again someday. You won't be back neither. You don't like it here."

"Where did you get that idea?" I laughed nervously. What Georgie said was true. I did plan to leave someday, but how did he know?

"Your dad, Mr. Trevor, he said you'd leave when he's gone. He said that."

"He's just worried. He shouldn't be."

"He said the paper man told him. You'll leave."

"Paper man? I'm the paper man," I laughed at him.

"The paper man where you worked. He called. He told Mr. Trevor." My amusement agitated him.

"Let's not talk about it now."

"Don't you like working with me, Mr. Mike?"

I winced as much from his apparent hurt as from his use of my nickname. "I like working with you very much." The truth was, I really did enjoy working with Georgie.

"Then why do you want to leave me? I — This is my job. If Mr. Trevor is gone, and you leave, I don't have a job. I don't have a family no more."

"Georgie, you have all kind of jobs. Everyone likes it when you work for them. Jesse wants you to work with him. The entire town is your family."

"But this is my job!" He spoke boldly. "My job is here. Your job is here. We work together. You, me, and Mr. Trevor, we're family."

"Let's not talk now," I repeated. "I'm late for the meeting."

"Mr. Trevor, he's ready."

"Mr. Trevor— Dad's not going. He needs to rest."

Georgie was right. Mr. Trevor was ready for the meeting and no amount of argument could persuade him otherwise. I tried to convince him that it was too cold, that his day had been long enough, that he needed to rest. In the end, I followed him out to the truck, and I waited until he was situated to drive toward town. Georgie sat in the back, his coat wrapped around him to keep warm. "Georgie told me you spoke to our old buddy in Detroit."

"Georgie has a big mouth," my father turned to look behind him. He smiled as the innocent man-child waved at him

"I haven't told Ted yet, but I've decided to stay."

"Yeah. We've played this game before."

"It's no game," I caused him to look at me. Only minutes before, I was sure that my words spoken to Georgie were lies. I can't say what changed my mind, but now as I sat in the truck with my father, I knew what I told him next was the truth. "I'm staying here. I'm running our paper, but it won't be the same paper we've run for years. I want to add some zing to it. Could you live with that?"

He still wasn't convinced. "So just what changed your mind?"

"It hasn't been one thing. It's been a dozen maybe more."

"The angels?"

"Angels abound in Serenity Key, don't they, Dad?"

"Yes, Michael, they do," he reached across the seat and patted my shoulder. "They sure do."

My father sat in the back of the small room known as the town hall. The place was packed, and upon first entering it was not clear whether support ran for or against Seth New. I moved up front to sit beside Turk Williams. The tall black man held out a hand in greeting. I shook it and sat beside him. Turk pointed to where Mickey was sitting next to a nervous Seth New. Mickey was conferencing with his very first "client." I brought a tape recorder, not wanting to miss one minute of what promised to be an exciting confrontation. The meeting commenced with the usual formalities and then the motion was drawn for removal of the current fire chief. Seth was called forward. He was accused of dereliction of duty and those against his remaining on duty stated their case. Seth listened intently, wincing when words were used like a sword to lash out at him. When their case was presented, Seth spoke. "I take full responsibility for all my actions," he said. "I stand before you a guilty man. Your trust in me has been broken. I apologize for my behavior, and I recognize that you have every right to remove me. You have seen me at my worst, and I have no valid excuse. I will accept the decision rendered here tonight."

There was stunned silence throughout the room. Without exception, everyone present expected more, much more from Seth. They came to the meeting to see a fight. Seth was disappointing them. He sat beside Mickey who placed a comforting hand on his shoulder.

"Chairman," a familiar voice rose from behind me. I watched as my father stepped forward.

"The council recognizes Trevor Abernathy."

Trevor stopped beside me. He placed a hand on my shoulder as he spoke. "I've known Seth New his entire life. I just listened to this young man show his true character, the same character I hope that my young man will exhibit if he is ever tried by life's circumstances. Responsibility is nothing that should be shrugged. What he did not say speaks louder to me than his words. Seth is willing to take responsibility for his actions, and he admits his faults. He didn't say he was sorry and then blame it on some outside circumstance. In today's society, this is a very rare trait, indeed."

My father's hand left my shoulder as he stepped forward. He stopped in front of Seth. "Life played a trick on this man that no one should have to face. Losing a spouse is never easy, especially when you're in the prime of life. It shook him. It shook him badly in just the same way it shook his father so many years ago when Seth's mother was lost, in just the same way it shook me when I lost my wife a couple of years ago. He reacted badly." Trevor chuckled to himself. "Does anyone remember how Jake reacted?" He turned to search the room for his old friend. "Jake ran my '57 Chevy so deep into the Gulf that it's a natural reef now." The entire room burst into laughter. "But once the initial grief wore off, Jake became one of our finest citizens. I'm still grieving for my car, by the way," he turned once again to Jake who shook his head. Then Trevor moved toward the podium facing the esteemed councilmen. "Seth's coming back to us. I've been watching him the past couple of days. I saw him today at the funeral of a dear friend. Most of you were there. Seth stood beside his good buddy Mickey in much the same way Mickey is standing beside him now, much the same way I stood beside his father way back when and the way his father has remained my true friend over the years." He turned back to Jake who stood now. "What would you have done without a second chance, Jake?"

"I would have died," Jake said honestly.

My father let the words sink in to the minds and conscience of those present. I realized that Trevor Abernathy's tongue was as sharp as his pen. He then turned back to the council. "Many of you have seen Seth on rescue day and night. He's a one-man team. He'd rather take the call than wake up some of the volunteers who have other jobs. I mean, he goes to help Old Eloise when she can't lift herself out of the chair because her husband is out cold on the sofa." Again, laughter rang out as Old Eloise confirmed that my father's statement was true.

I watched as he gripped the podium so tightly his knuckled turned white. "Even in the pit of his despair, Seth New came to my house and rescued me from sure death. He provided me with the CPR that brought me back from my first heart attack, and the second one." The hairs on the back of my neck stood. I looked to Seth who stared at me, at Mickey who offered me a sympathetic look.

"We know when we call that he'll be there. You offer complaints against him, but he has never once failed to appear when called." My father's right fist pounded the podium while his left hand still gripped it tightly. He bent forward as if in pain. I rose. He straightened.

"Mr. Trevor," Georgie's anguished voice sounded from behind me.

My father raised his hand to summon his silence. "There's much talk about the angels that appear suddenly for some reason or other, their messages from God attached. Angels..." He hesitated, bent again, and forced himself straight. Seth was on his feet. "My son has spent a great deal of time looking for the purpose of angels, and in the Christmas Eve edition of his paper, he'll tell you what he considers to be the Biblical reasons for our invisible friends that we wrongly envision with wings and halos. He'll tell you God's angels send us messages; they protect us in realms unseen and in ways that we barely notice, a gentle nudge, a little urging to do something we might not normally do. He'll tell you they offer comfort and encouragement." Again he fell silent, looked at each member of the council then he turned to me. "I'm sorry, Michael, angels are messengers. It is God who is our protector, our hope, and our encouragement. It is God that commands His angels. They may give us gentle reminders and provide protection in realms unseen." He looked around the room, each person silent, unmoving, clinging to his every word, "Folks, without God's command they cannot act." He was silent for a long moment before turning his attention back to the council members. "You must remember that offering compassion, encouragement and protection, these things aren't impossible for us, especially when Jesus fulfills his promise and resides within us. When John bowed down to the angel, he writes in Revelation 22:9 that the angel warned, '...See thou do it not: for I am thy fellowservant, and of thy brethren the prophets, and of them which keep the sayings of this book: worship God.'" He turned his eyes to Seth. His words were meant to be a strong message for my friend. "Worship God," he repeated before looking to the council once again. "As Christians, whom many of us have professed to be, we have more power than all the angels, through Jesus," he stopped, his body rigid. His voice strangled. He struggled to recover. "And we have one power over them. We can forgive and we know through God's word that we should be faithful in forgiveness. After all, he is faithful in forgiving us." He turned away from the podium, slow and unsteady. I stepped toward him. "Michael," he called my name just before he collapsed into my arms.

Chapter Nine

Gratitude Returned

"Many waters cannot quench love, neither can the floods
drown it: if a man would give all the substance of his house
for love, it would utterly be contemned." - Song of Solomon 8:7

The Christmas Eve edition of the *Serenity Serenade* remained
unprinted. Instead of running the press and delivering the paper, I sat
by my father's hospital bed. Mickey and Sandy Roberts stepped out
into the hall with Blanchie, and I sat alone. The door opened, and I
turned. Seth motioned for me to stay seated as he stood beside me.
"He's a fighter," he spoke. Seth remained at the hospital since our
arrival. He had been with Georgie most of the time until Turk
Williams insisted on taking the exhausted man-child home with him.

Seth had revived my father for what appeared the third time since
his heart began to fail. He had, in his expertise, gotten my father to
the hospital alive. "I've got to have the chance to tell him that he
didn't have to go this far to prove I deserved another chance." His
words were meant to be humorous, to provide me with some relief,
but they hung between us.

"I didn't think he was a fighter," I confessed. "I accused him of giving up."

"Not Trevor. He tried to run the paper. My dad even tried to help,
but it just became too much even with both of them working it."

"No one ever told me."

"He didn't want you to know."

94

"I don't understand," I lowered my head. "I was the one who should have known."

"Michael," my father's voice was weak.

"I'm here," I reached for his hand.

"I don't want you to hold on to the grief like you did with your mother," his voice was hoarse. "Let me go. I won't be alone."

Selfishly, I wanted to scream at him, tell him I would be alone. I didn't want to be alone.

It was Seth's hand on my shoulder that reminded me that I was not by myself. I nodded to my father, tried to keep the tears from stinging my eyes.

"Make sure you sell the paper to the right person."

"I won't be selling the paper. I told you that."

"You can stop that right now," he seemed to grow stronger just to scold me. "I know you're going back to Detroit."

"I'm giving my notice, Dad. You showed me there is adventure here. I'm going to keep searching."

"Michael, do you know what causes us to grieve the most?"

"Loss," I answered.

"Not exactly," he surprised me. "Guilt, thinking we should or could have done so much more for the person we lost. So, don't you grieve for me, son. You have nothing to regret."

I nodded, "I'm staying anyway."

I saw the genuine relief on his face. "Take care of Georgie. I've never said it, but I love him like my brother. God used him to fill Carl's place."

I never realized that, but looking back over the last couple of weeks, I knew it was true. He and Georgie were close friends, and my father loved being there for the man-child. "Dad?"

He turned his head toward me.

"How'd you do it?"

"What?"

"The angels. I know it was you. Where did they come from?"

He smiled. "I knew you were a real reporter. When did you figure it out?"

"When I started getting the calls, putting the colors in categories. It took awhile, but when you quoted to the council from Revelation I realized you were the only one it could be."

"There it is?" He looked at Seth.

"What, Mr. Abernathy?" Seth inquired.

"That college education at work," he used the tired old joke, but it made Seth laugh.

"But where? How? Why?" I asked the three questions that in the beginning were so important.

"There were only a few, thirty or so. Your mother — It was her idea. She tatted them intending to give them away as an encouragement to others." He closed his eyes tightly to await the passing of the pain. "I found them, and I began to give them away."

"The colors?"

"She told me about them, and I found a note she wrote so she wouldn't forget their meanings."

"How did you do it?"

"Georgie," he solved the mystery. "Georgie delivered them." I smiled and shook my head. Hadn't I even commented to Sandy that nothing got past Georgie? He would be the one to know all that was going on in the lives of the people in our little town.

"The red one, was it to throw me off?"

A smile again parted his dry lips. "It was for you, Michael. It was the last angel your mother made. She was planning to give it to you when you graduated from college. She made it red as a symbol of our love, hers and mine toward you, and red to remind you of God's love for you, and red to remind you that the power of love cannot be diminished." He gripped my hand. Still, I could feel his strength ebbing. "I love you. You have always made me proud, always." His words were soft. I bowed my head. My tears fell on the sheets of his bed. His hold on my hand lessened, and I took a trembling breath. It was then that I knew. I looked around the room.

"What's wrong?" Seth was concerned.

"Momma?" I spoke to the emptiness around us. I still felt her presence. It was the same comfort I knew as a child when I laid with a fever in bed, too sick to raise my head. I would look up, and she would be there beside me, and I felt safe and loved.

It was sometime before I could look to my father's face, and it was Seth who told me what I suspected. "He's gone, Michael." He had slipped away from me as quietly and as peacefully as Sabrina Roberts left her family once she was released. Seth left the room quietly. I was alone with my grief, and I sat beside my father holding his hand until I knew I had to leave him.

"I'm sorry," Mickey was the first by my side.

I bit my lip trying to summon the courage to speak without showing too much of my emotions. "You know when you told me that you felt your father's presence before your mother died?"

Mickey nodded.

"I felt Momma's presence. Mickey, I don't believe that kind of comfort was meant for Sabrina or for my father."

"I don't understand."

"I believe without a doubt that Jesus shows us the way home. Sabrina and Trevor left us in complete peace because He was with them. God knew what would comfort us the most. He gave us the remembrance of those we loved to make it easier to let them go. It's just a theory."

Mickey went with me as I made the funeral arrangements, and then he drove me home. Until he left, I felt no loneliness, but as he drove away, I felt as if I were the only one in the entire world. The house was dark as I entered. The phone rang, and I answered. "Dead," I replied. "He's dead." I lowered the receiver and sat with it in my hand for a long while until the knock at the door. I forced myself up and opened it. I was engulfed first in the arms of Sally Williams who then allowed Bella Edwards and her Aunt Rosa to hold me in my sadness. It was not long before the house filled with people who wanted nothing more than to comfort me. I was not alone. I would never be alone in Serenity Key. I would never be leaving Serenity Key. It is my home, and its people are filled with more life and love than anywhere on earth.

My guests left in the early morning, and I slept late on Christmas day. It never once dawned on me in my grief that my friends willingly sacrificed Christmas Eve with their families to provide me with comfort. I pulled myself from bed fueled by the memory of my promise to my father that I would not hold on to my pain. I wanted to be productive.

I started walking toward the paper office where Georgie met me. His face was red from crying. "Mr. Trevor's gone?"

"Mr. Trevor's gone," I placed my arm around him. "Where were you last night?"

"I was sad."

"Mr. Trevor doesn't want us to be sad. He wants us to work," I stopped. He faced me. "He wants us to work together, Georgie, me and you, on his paper. It means a lot of work. It means I have to teach you new things. Is that what you want?"

"I want what Mr. Trevor wants."

"Good." We started our walk. "Then buck up, and let's go do just that."

There was not much to do. I didn't plan on a big issue. Having missed the Christmas Eve deadline, I had just three items I wanted to place on the two-page edition. The first was my father's last byline. I listened over and over again to the tape I recorded at the council meeting, and when I had my father's speech down line for line I printed it. It stood both as my story about the angels and the coverage of the meeting. The article held one column while my father's obituary filled the other. On the back page of the paper, Georgie and I wished everyone a Happy New Year, and Georgie was officially made a part of the *Serenity Serenade* fulfilling my father's wishes.

Once finished, I spent most of my time with the man-child. I wanted to be beside him, help him understand my father's passing. "He said he loved you like a brother," I told him. "That makes us family."

"I'm your Uncle Georgie. You call me Uncle Georgie?"

"Sure Uncle Georgie." I teased hoping he would forget, knowing he would not.

"I like that. I will take care of you now since Mr. Trevor's gone."

"I want you to sit beside me at the funeral. Will you do that?"

He nodded. I sent him home to rest. The funeral would be held the next morning, and I found that I did want time alone. I sat in the office remembering a childhood spent with the old machinery and the words that formed in my imagination. I thought of my mother's angels and the special love they spread since her death. I reflected on my father's faith and my lack thereof. My father had been too ill to attend church, but he remained faithful in his reading of the Scriptures. He had shared his faith with others through the angels. Not once since my return did the thought of attending a church service enter my mind, even though my attention did turn a time or two to my faith.

"Many waters cannot quench love, neither can floods drown it: if a man would give all the substance of his house for love, it would utterly be contemned." The words ran through my mind. I now understood them completely. I knew why they were meant for me. I was encompassed by love and warmth my entire life. My parents always surrounded me with comfort and peace and hope. My friends provided me with true companionship. I gave love all of my life, and in all but one instance it had been returned to me overflowing and unbound. Nothing ever quenched that love, not disappointment, not time, or space, or anyone. Tears could not drown the love. It could not be destroyed by failure. My heart, my soul, saved by Christ himself, was within my body and Christ was a resident there. No matter how much I gave of my heart, my soul, it could not be destroyed. It could not be left condemned.

It was true. My mother was gone. My father had departed, but their love lived on. I held it very close, but I was very willing to share. It was given to me, and even if I tried, I could not give away all of it. It was steadfast and sure. It was sound and true.

"For I am persuaded, that neither death, nor life, nor angels, nor principalities, nor powers, nor things present, nor things to come, nor height, nor depth, nor any other creature, shall be able to separate us from the love of God, which is in Christ Jesus our Lord." I paced as I said the verses, Romans 8:38 and 39, aloud. Sabrina Roberts shared her love with us by teaching. I knew those were her favorite verses, and I knew they meant something to her, but as I fell to my knees and bowed my head, I knew they also had a meaning for me. I walked away from Jesus just as assuredly as I walked away from my father. Jesus, like my father, never abandoned me. My father hoped I would come back to him, but Jesus knew I would return to His side. I repented for my backsliding and my doubt, and I asked Jesus to show me what it was he meant for me to do.

I must have been on my knees before the Lord for hours. I prayed like I never prayed before. Verses began to come to mind. I petitioned God to have His will with Blanchie and Jesse Crum. I remembered Jesse's request that day in front of the Roberts' houses, and I asked God to visit him, to make his life uncomfortable and cause a change to occur. I asked that He protect Jesse's father on the missionary field. I prayed for the new born babies in our community, for health, love and guidance. I prayed for Valley and Brad Rasneck. I prayed that Seth find this same hope and peace, and I prayed strength for Hannah Miller. I prayed for Jake New's business and for Noah McGowan's new position as pastor. I asked the Lord to bless his upcoming marriage to beautiful Bella Edwards and strengthen their faith even more.

I did not want to leave His presence. It took so long for me to return to it and I welcomed His comfort. I thanked him for my friendship with Georgie and with Mickey and Sandy. I thanked him for my new acquaintance with Turk and Sally Williams and my renewal of friendship with Curt Davis. I prayed that the friendship he knew with Noah would return as strong as my friendship with Mickey. "I love you, Father," I said aloud, and my heart seemed to grow. I felt as if my soul would burst. "I love you because you have never stopped loving me." I remained, head bowed, for some time until I knew it was time to rise. "You are an awesome God."

I was surprised that His comfort did not leave me. I left the *Serenade* office and walked home. The phone rang and I was invited to join Turk and Sally Williams at their home for Christmas dinner with Sandy and Mickey Roberts. Curt, I was told, had other plans, and I remembered he did have an aunt who lived on the island and perhaps his friend, Lonnie Culver, would join them. One the way to the Williams' house, I picked up my "uncle" who was also invited to dinner.

A few days later, and for the second time in less than two weeks, Serenity Key natives piled into the Serenity Key Baptist Church. They were provided with a copy of the *Serenade* as they entered, and while Georgie and I sat in the front of the church we could hear the familiar rustle of the pages, and the murmur of surprise as they read that portion of my father's obituary that revealed his responsibility for the angels.

Noah McGowan came to stand in front of me. "I have to tell you, I prayed most of the night that God would make this easy for me," he confessed. "And he did. Thank you for the paper."

"It was my last gift to him," I shook his hand. "Thank you, Noah. I know you never thought your first sermon would be given at a funeral."

"At least I knew him well," he reached over and shook Georgie's hand. "How are you doing?"

"Fine." Georgie blubbered beside me, and I slipped my arm around him to provide him comfort. "It's okay, you know," I spoke as Noah moved away. "He's not in that box. He's with Jesus and Ms. Claire. Ms. Roberts is with them, too. We should be happy for him." Then I remembered the words that helped me so much after the death of my mother. "Georgie, we'll always have the memories he left for us. Every time we run that paper, a part of him is there beside us."

Georgie nodded. "I loved Mr. Trevor."

"I know you did. That's why you're here with me."

I leaned against him and turned to look where the open casket set. I blinked my own tears away. I thought of my mother's funeral and the devastation I felt at that time. I thanked God that I had been brought to understand His love and His will in my life.

Noah McGowan was generous as he provided an expose on my father's past, his love, and his kindness. He spoke about the community and how my father's love for it was shown through the *Serenade*. He reminded everyone that Trevor's death was simply a graduation from this life into the rest of eternity. He shared with us the fact that Christ was my father's savior and that by simply believing and asking the Lord, he would be our savior also.

When Noah finished speaking, my father's best friend stood before the mourners, his back to them for several minutes. When Jake turned around, his eyes were on me. "God blessed that man." He spoke the words that were so similar to those spoken by Sally Williams, and I recognized her "amen" from somewhere behind.

"Everything he did was for you, you know?" He spoke to me. I nodded. "He loved you very much." Jake did it. He brought the tears I was fighting to my eyes. I nodded again. "What a remarkable man," he continued. "In silence he suffered with real heart disease while bringing to the attention of many the disease of our hearts. He did it for me so many years ago, so many times. He did it for my son. Trevor Abernathy was a quiet man who lived on a quaint island. He came from a big city to escape the depravity of society. When he first came here I remember my own father saying that things would change. With a big city newspaperman we would have skeletons out of our closets before we knew it. Well, I'll tell you that scared me. I have too many of those skeletons, and I sure didn't want them being rattled around by some know-it-all from the big city." There was tearful laughter. "But even my father had to admit after awhile that Trevor was meant for Serenity Key and his *Serenade* belonged to all of us. Trevor wasn't here to dig up secrets. He was here to share his gift with words. God used Trevor Abernathy. He placed him in our midst and used him like a beacon even though I'm not quite sure he even recognized it. God, through Trevor, brought to each of us love, comfort, gentle reminders, protection, and He did it all through a collection of tatted angels left by a woman of extraordinary love and compassion. Serenity Key will miss him just as we have missed Claire, but he left us someone who, like his father, has proven to be just as good a friend to all of us. I repeat, God blessed that man, and God bless you, Michael." He stepped down, shook my hand and patted Georgie on the shoulder. The music played, and while Georgie and I sat, my father's friends filed past us to pay their respects. Georgie and I were the last to leave the sanctuary because the man my father considered his brother, cried as if he lost his only friend in the world.

It was at the grave where Georgie and I sat, listening again to Noah as he spoke about life after death, that I felt my greatest loss, that of a good, good friend, someone who stood beside me in all my decisions and allowed me to find my way. I closed my eyes and asked God for his strength and his guidance. I did not hear Noah close the service. When I lifted my eyes, I looked up into my best friend's face. Mickey smiled as he reached out his hand and handed me the tatted angel that belonged to his mother. As he stepped past, his wife held out the rose angel, the one given to Mickey for his loss. This was their way of returning the gratitude Sabrina Roberts wanted to voice to my father but had been unable to give. Blanchie and Jesse Crum followed. Each laid their green angel in my lap. Next, Turk and Sally stood in front of us. "Take good care of her." Turk's low voice spoke to Georgie who simply nodded. Turk's large hand rested against Georgie's face as if he were a child. "It's okay." He enveloped Georgie as the man-child stood and cried against him. Seth came by with Hannah at his side. He handed me his angel in rose. "I was afraid to clean her up." His eyes were moist. "But she's still beautiful."

I nodded, and when the service was done, and the mourners were walking back to their cars, between us, Georgie and I held thirty-two angels of rose, green, blue and yellow. I was comforted in my loss, protected from my fears, and reminded that in Serenity Key I had a home with many friends. Still there was one other angel. The thirty-third sat at home, the only red angel, given to me by the two people who loved me enough to let me discover on my own that Jesus loves me so much more.

Afterword

Dear Readers:

When my husband first read this story, he commented that there were too many deaths involved for one small town. I took his words to heart, and I began to think of a way to lessen the cold, hard fact that deaths happen and that they cause pain, inescapable sorrow, and in many cases a feeling of utter devastation. It was at that point that I realized why God allowed this book to be written.

By the time I turned thirty-one, I had suffered through the loss of several people I loved. So deep was my sorrow, that I believe events in my life were dictated by my refusal to deal with their loss.

When you're nineteen, you believe you'll live forever. You always think there's time to keep up with friends, and if it's not this year you'll contact them the next. Conrad came into my life twice, each for brief periods of time. When we were twelve years old, he lived next to my grandmother's home, and he became my friend. He was a mischievous kid, but his nature was as sweet as honey. My clearest memory of Conrad was catching the bus to attend Sunday school and church at the local Baptist church. To this day, I can't tell you if we attended once or many times, but I do remember that particular Sunday when the invitation was given, and both Conrad and I walked the aisle toward the pastor and accepted Christ as our savior. As I said, we were only twelve at the time, and I don't know if Conrad ever went to that church again. I don't know anything about his relationship with God. For that matter, he never knew of mine.

Conrad moved away attending school out of state for a while, and I did not see him again until we were both very young adults. Our renewed friendship at that time was brief, but Conrad was never far from my thoughts. So, on the day when I turned on the news at Noon and the reporter announced that there had been a traffic accident in which three local teens (young adults) were injured, I joked to myself that someone I knew was in an accident. The woman's next words pounded into my heart, and my reaction and the way they made me feel are as vivid to me today as they were twenty years ago. When she pronounced Conrad's death, my breath caught in my throat, my knees failed me, and I fell to the ground.

I suffered my pain alone. I didn't attend the small service his mother gave. I didn't call that dear woman and tell her how sorry I was for her loss. Very few people knew how I actually felt about this young man. You see I came to realize that I was not "in love" with Conrad. I loved him dearly. Until this writing, I could count the number of people who knew how much I missed him. I held it deeply inside.

Three days before my twenty-third birthday, I lost the woman I loved more than any being on this earth. Grandmothers are supposed to love and spoil their grandchildren, but my Grandma did much more than that. She sheltered me, she encouraged me, and she provided so much more than material goods. Her love for me was unconditional. Her loss was made even more painful by my own actions.

I can't describe the closeness we shared during all those years of my youth, but I can tell you, that as I grew older, I grew away from her. It was not an emotional parting. It was a physical one. I didn't visit as much as I should. I didn't provide the same love and devotion she had given to me when I needed it most. So, when the call came that told me I was needed at the hospital immediately, I was taken by surprise.

It wasn't long after I reached the hospital, not long after the phone was placed to her ear so that she could hear my father's voice, that Elizabeth Fay Thompson, left this world, and left me feeling so alone and so angry with myself for letting her down.

My relationship with my mother was the exact opposite of the one I enjoyed with my grandmother. She was a difficult woman, and I was a stubborn child. Add to the mix that we were mother and daughter, and you have a volatile mixture of love and hate. Oh, Colleen

Thompson did not hate me. The trouble was, I believed she loved me too much, and I was forever trying to pull away from that love.

Our relationship was so complicated and filled with emotion, that it is only now, nine years after her death that I can appreciate who she was and what she did for me. My mother never graduated high school. She received her GED when I was in high school, and it was one of the proudest days of her life. For a short time, we also attended junior college together. She worked for a convenience store chain for more than fourteen years, most of those years following a robbery in which she was shot in the face. I look back now, and I cannot fathom how she raised two daughters, owned a home, and had a vehicle on the wages she brought home.

I know how long she worked at the convenience stores because I remember clearly what caused her to quit her job and give up on life. It was the prison release of the man who shot her and his arrival at our home to finish the job. It was then that my mother suffered a nervous breakdown and gave up on life. She tried to keep going, but from that time on, she had made up her mind that she was going to die.

So many times she told me that she wouldn't live much longer that I began to ignore her. She was diagnosed with emphysema probably before she stopped working, and although it was slowly taking her away, it wasn't fast enough for her.

That's why on the day I received the call at work that told me I was needed at the hospital right away, I was unprepared for what awaited me. My aunts and uncles were there. Our pastor was called, but I just could not believe that these were to be her final hours.

After my family left, after the pastor spoke to my mother, and when darkness came, I stayed beside her bed. I held her hand. For a woman who was ready to die for so many years, it became evident to me that she was fighting sleep. She knew and I knew that if she closed her eyes, she would drift away from me forever.

As she cried out in pain throughout the night, I sat beside her. I couldn't believe that it came down to this. All our years of fighting, all my teenage rebellion, and in her final hours, I couldn't have left her for all the money in the world.

Toward morning, she was exhausted, I was worn out, and all I could do was pray. I remember accepting the fact that she wasn't going to pull out of this one and surprise us all, and it was at that time, that I bowed my head. Foolish prayers come to you in times of great need, and they sound so profound. I bowed my head and prayed that the Lord would send my mother's father to show her the way home.

It was at that same time that an old familiar feeling came upon me. It was as if I sensed my grandmother's presence at my side. My mother was very close to my father's mother. So, immediately, I assumed that the Lord had allowed my grandmother to show my mother the way Home.

When moments later, my sister walked through the door, she said good morning, and I returned her greeting. To our surprise, Mom spoke clearly, and it was so plain that she was joking with us, "You shut up," she said. She was ready for sleep, and because she seldom used that humorous tone, I responded in kind.

"Don't you tell me to shut up," I teased, and as my sister and I watched, our mother took her last breath.

I remember an overwhelming sense of calm. I was able to stand and call for the nurse. I was able to hold my sister against me and tell her that she was just gone from her body. Mom was with the Lord.

There are two scenes in this book that reflect my experience during my mother's death. It wasn't until writing this story that I realized that the Lord is not going to send others to bring his loved ones home. My mother was ready to leave this world because he was the one holding out his hand to her. With all my heart, I know that I was given a remembrance to make my mother's going easier for me.

All this to say that when I began this quaint little tale, it was a story to show that angels, God's creation, do not have halos and wings. God, though, had a different idea all together, for when I put the final period on the last page, I knew that God had used this work to speak directly into my grief and to begin filling those holes that loss created.

It is my sincere hope and prayer that it has done the same for you. Please write and share your thoughts with me.

FayLamb (mclamb@sprynet.com)
October 30, 2000